FISHING with JOEY

A Memoir of My Marine Son

THOMAS LOGAN

Copyright © 2025 by **Thomas Logan/The Red Lions Project**

All rights reserved. No portion of this publication may be reproduced, stored in an electronic system, or transmitted in any form by any means, electronic, mechanical, photocopy, recording, or otherwise, without the author's prior permission, except with brief quotations used in literary reviews and specific non-commercial uses permitted by copyright law. Please use the contact information at the back of this book for permission requests.

The views expressed in this book are the author's and do not necessarily reflect those of the publisher.

Scripture references marked as "NIV" are taken from the New International Version. Holy Bible, New International Version®, NIV® Copyright ©1973, 1978, 1984, 2011 by Biblica, Inc. ® Used by permission. All rights reserved worldwide.

Cover and Interior Layout by 2025 Harvest Creek Publishing and Design
www.harvestcreek.net

Ordering Information: Churches, associations, and others can receive special discounts on quantity purchases. For details, please contact the author at the email address listed in the author section at the back of the book.

Fishing With Joey—1st ed.

ISBN: 978-1-961641-29-7

Printed in The United States of America

Contents

Preface 7

Foreword 11

The Trail of Ashes 17

The Trail of Ashes Continues 29

The Trail Leads to Montana 37

The Trail to the White River in Arkansas 51

Montana—The Sundown Mission 55

MAKING MEMORIES WITH MY SON 59

Joey Had Balls 61

Arkansas: White River Fishing Trip 67

Back to Camp 75

White Hole on the River 79

Riding the Surge on the White River 81

Big Horn and Big Bull Moose 83

Black Canyon 87

Charlie and Joey 91

Get Lost in Montana 93

Sun Valley, Idaho—The Big Wood River 97

The Lochsa River 101

Old Faithful in Yellowstone 107

Our Oasis in the Desert 113

The Old Man River 117

Camping On the Journey 119

SHATTERED HOPES AND DREAMS 121

Hog Wild 123

Our Last Phone Call.. 125

Plane Ride to Dover AFB.. 131

Too Little, Too Late 135

90th Floor... 139

The Flag Flown Over Washington 141

Arlington 143

Sikorsky—W.W.N.F. 149

The Lioness in the Darkness 153

Over We Go!.. 155

Faith in God 159

The Red Lion Flag.. 161

An Unexpected Gift 165

UNDERSTANDING THE TRUE VALUE OF TREASURED MEMORIES 167

A Surprise Thank-You Card 169

The ReNaming of a Bridge 171

Two Cigars... 173

Troutaholic Sunday 175

Two Owls... 177

Little Big Horn 179

A Vision from Heaven 181

The Rose Garden 185

Two Pictures, Two Thousand Words... 187

Veteran's Day 193

Ruger Red Lion Pistol... 197

Six Coffee Mugs... 199

The Miraculous Yellow Rose 201

The Soldier's Cross 203

Flying High with Nike Air 205

Grandpa Guiseppe Cioci... 209

Joey's 1940 Chevy.. 213

The Red Lion Colt .45 Auto Pistol 215

LeTourneau University... 225

Darkness in Montana 229

Heaven's Gate 231

The Birth of a Miracle... 233

Blue Balloons 237

The Cap and the Mug 241

Two Women, Two Paintings 241

A Special Email.. 249

The Fallen Six Memorial from Afghanistan............................... 253

The H.E.A.R.T.S. Museum 255

Home of the Brave Quilt 257

Kind Words from the Commander... 261

Extended Memories 267
About the Author 279

Preface

NO ONE WILLINGLY chooses to become part of the Gold Star Families. That is reserved for family members of those who have died in the line of duty or while in service to their country. The membership "cost" is an immense amount of pain and sorrow.

My wife and I would never have expected to join this group, although there are generations of military veterans in our family. And with me being a retired police officer, I had certainly seen it all. However, I never imagined the possibility of losing a family member in war.

It's possible that my time in law enforcement caused me to become desensitized to the pain and suffering that families experience. Like most parents, I had hopes and dreams for each of our children. So, I never even considered that those dreams might be shattered. But that chilling knock on the door one fateful night changed our lives forever.

My son, Joey, was gone in an instant. Sadly, his life was cut short just weeks before he was scheduled to return home. He never got the chance to fulfill his ambitions or explore the numerous dreams that constantly bubbled up in his imaginative brain.

In retrospect, I think I saw this coming. Call it fate, faith, or even just a father's simple intuition, but somehow, deep down, I knew that Joey might not return home. And so, the summer before he went off to boot camp, we took a trip that any father and son would only dream of.

Our time together was almost too good to be true. Oh, don't get me wrong—we had our typical father/son moments! However, it was also an amazingly wonderful time. While we chased the best fishing spots throughout the country, my wife ensured our bank account remained full.

Our primary responsibility was keeping the lures intact and observing the map carefully while traveling.

Mornings were dedicated to preparing our tackle for the day's big catch, while evenings were spent sharing stories around the campfire. It was something I will never regret. This opportunity allowed me to connect with my son in a way I never thought possible.

Fishing with Joey serves many purposes. First, it is a physical account of the days before, during, and following Joey's death. In a way, recording them in a book has been therapeutic while dealing with profound grief. It has also been a reminder to me that life is good, even when things are tough. I never want to forget the special moments we shared on our trip.

But the book also highlights the kindness of the human spirit, which shines through—even in our darkest hour. Hundreds, if not thousands, of people have stood with our family as we have walked this road of loss. Both prominent figures and ordinary individuals have provided their incredible support. Personally, I've come to believe that the many stories you'll read are not mere coincidences, but part of a divine plan meant to guide us and honor our son's life.

This book is divided into three sections:

- First, tall tales from the wonderful summer when Joey and I got to share our love of fishing.
- Next, the tremendous shock and shattered memories we experienced following his death.
- Finally, stories of restored hope and recovery, a testament to the support of our community and larger family.

Throughout all of this, there is one common thread. My son's bright and joyous spirit motivates me to keep pushing forward. His memory motivates me to rise each morning and also inspires our family's work in creating a lasting tribute to him through the Red Lions Project.

As a reader, please know that the book's profits will be used to commemorate our son and the other fallen heroes of the HMH-363 Red Lions. Joey's dream of creating a Montana Retreat Center with woodland cabins where veterans could find peace and "decompress" after their tour of duty has become a reality. We hope it will be a place to welcome veterans for many years to come. For more information about the project, visit www.redlionproject.org.

Semper Fi to all who are faithfully protecting our nation.
Thomas Logan

Foreword

For no one is cast off by the Lord forever,
Though he brings grief, he will show compassion,
so great is his unfailing love.
For he does not willingly bring affliction
or grief to anyone.
LAMENTATIONS 3:31-33 (NIV)

THERE IS A CERTAIN surrealism to the prospect of finding something truly remarkable right under your very nose. A gem that is hidden just under the surface of the sand. A profound piece of wisdom that you have heard all your life but never quite appreciated or fully understood. *A man who has lived a fascinating life that you knew absolutely nothing about despite having been your next-door neighbor for over 20 years.*

I found myself in this circumstance, becoming more acquainted with Tom Logan. Whether Providence or happenstance brought me outside for a walk with my dogs on a drizzled mid-April day ultimately matters not, though I would like to believe it was the workings of the former. *I am truly grateful.*

I had known Tom, his son Joey, and the few members of his family who had infrequently come to our doorstep or appeared across our lots, only in passing. Joey and I had gone to the same schools together but had different friend circles, which was normal for boys two years apart with different personalities and diverging interests. His best friend had romanced my cousin for a short spell, and I shared several classes with his sister. Tom and his wife, Debi, who moved to our area shortly after my family built our house, were both police officers from Houston.

Other than these tidbits, I knew next to nothing about the mysterious Logans, who mostly kept to themselves and were rarely seen except at their frequent bonfire gatherings. So, imagine my surprise when I noticed the patriarch himself standing at the edge of his driveway on a grey, rainy day, his eyes locked onto me.

I had spoken to Tom on a few occasions over the years, mowed his yard as a favor a few times, met his grandchildren, and attended his son's funeral. But, as I stopped and greeted him, it became immediately apparent that this meeting would be vastly different from the rest. In an instant, it became clear to me that I had a much deeper understanding of this man. Something just clicked with him, and just like that, the quiet, grizzled old man next door became like a book one could not put down. A brief walk down the block transformed into a captivating four-hour conversation on Midway Drive.

It turns out we have numerous shared interests. We both shared a love of hunting and the wilderness, a fascination with the glory of the Old West and the Civil War, a desire to read the captivating stories of history, the military, and survivalism, a hobby of woodworking and crafts that brought much joy, and probably most of all: our fascination with vintage and antique firearms.

It was this, at first, that kept me coming back to spend hours upon hours in the War Room, discussing everything from the Battle of Little Bighorn to Bigfoot. I began to notice a myriad of seemingly random items plastered over every inch of wall space. But they were not without purpose or design. In due time, I would learn the verse each one of them contributed to the epic poem that was the life of Tom Logan.

Tom was from New York (which explained why I could never quite put my finger on why he sounded different from the rest of us all those years). He had been an armorer and a marksmanship instructor in the Air Force and later a cop in more departments than would have seemed possible to me. He possessed a deep love of fishing, in particular, a love that he had instilled into his son. He made his own fishing and fly rods as a hobby, purely for its own sake, and later, to connect and give comfort to disabled combat veterans. He even made an exquisite USMC-themed rod as a memorial for his fallen fishing partner.

He and Joey had done it all together: hunting, fishing, hiking, camping, shooting. They were outdoorsmen through and through; I likened them to a couple of humble, modern-day Teddy Roosevelts, seeing as they had stories of a similar tone and equal caliber. But when Tom recounted the tale of his and Joey's three-month, 16,000-mile trip up through the Rockies, Montana, Canada, and back, I vehemently suggested he write a book.

Before I knew it, an entire filing cabinet's worth of documents was at my feet: Manuscripts, folders, notebooks, and pictures. Tom had been journaling vigorously since the day of the tragedy, compiling a detailed account of all the memories he had accrued, from before Joey had left to after he was gone. He had been trying to find editors to help organize and eventually publish this collection, Tom's own version of *War and Peace,* as he sardonically called it. After several severely disappointing attempts, he resigned to give up the endeavor. Not quite realizing what I had gotten myself into, I told him that I would take on the project. *I do not regret it in the slightest.*

Thinking back on it, I *had* to do this. I was there when Joey's motorcade drove by our home, then nine years back. Our unknown town was suddenly flooded with attention from the national media, veterans' organizations, federal politicians, and even the infamous Westboro Baptists. Our town was so unknown that even people living 50 miles away had never heard of it. And yet, all of it was done for one Marine, who none of them knew, as well as the innumerable acts of kindness that followed.

It had always struck me that there was something special about this one. By then, most of the flag-waving displays of patriotism and celebrations of veterans returning home, alive or otherwise, had long faded away. Joseph Daniel Logan was not some famous general, and he certainly was not the first Marine to perish in a war that had just entered its ninth year. He was just another helicopter gunner, one of countless others. Outside our little town, he was no one; just another faceless name from East-Jesus Nowhere, Texas, in a long list of casualties in some Pentagon filing cabinet somewhere or on a marble plaque in Arlington. Or, at least, that would have been the logical assumption. But it didn't appear that way.

I have a deep appreciation for the written word and a repressed desire to fancy myself as a writer, so the project appealed to me from the outset. But I soon realized it was far more than that. I was being entrusted to tenderly handle and organize the scattered, cherished memories a father had of his beloved son, of a life lost that I now deeply regret not having been a part of from the moment they planted roots right next door.

It's painful in the sense of knowing that Joey and I could have been close friends for a dozen reasons had I simply walked over and started up a conversation. Well, now I get my second chance, not the way it should have been, but with an equally compelling and noble man whom I now consider a close friend and mentor. It has been an honor and a privilege to be a part of something bigger than myself and to pay due respect to a great man who so clearly touched the lives of not only his fellow servicemen but countless souls around this great nation.

In keeping with Tom's desires and the nature of his writing style and subject matter, I have endeavored to be as unintrusive as absolutely possible. These are the personal journal entries of a convalescent man, and we decided it best to retain their essences as they are for the purposes of healing and inspiration. In my own opinion, I have grown fond of Tom's straightforward, everyman style of writing. It not only conveys authenticity but paints an uplifting image of a merciful God inclined to wink, a bygone time whose values are still contemporaneous, a nation that people still have pride in if one looks closely enough at the indomitable human spirit, and the inexhaustible kindness of Smalltown, USA.

Corey Wood, a family friend

Only our individual faith

in Freedom

can keep us free.
—Dwight D. Eisenhower

The Trail of Ashes

OUR LIFE TOOK A TURN on January 19, 2012. That's the day my wife Debi, who is Joey's mother and my best friend, and I received the devastating news of our son's death. He died in Afghanistan when the helicopter he was flying in crashed in the Hindu Kush mountains.

The entire crew went down with no survivors—six brave Marines gone in the blink of an eye. Two Marines came to the door that night to tell us what had happened. Their helicopter had fallen from 4,000 feet, then exploded into a ball of fire. No one could help them. This memory will stay etched in my mind forever.

Joey loved the Marine Corps and loved flying even more. His fellow Marines told me he would often ask them to fly their missions. And when he wasn't on the flight schedule, he would get mad and ask the C.O. to fly him. I found out later that he was the most-flown observer in his unit for this deployment.

Our son had left home three years before and had become an outstanding young man. I really did not know the potential he had until after that fateful day. God had other plans for him and his crewmembers, and in the same way, it has inspired me to do things I thought were impossible.

Debi and I are coping with our loss each in our own way; so far, she is the strong one. Joey would have told me to quit being such a girl about it. That's what the Marines call each other when they are feeling sorry for themselves. I'm getting better, and I know he is looking over my shoulder, giving me a shove occasionally. A lot has happened since Joey's passing. Our *trail of ashes* has been a soul-searching experience that has taught me a lot of things about life and how little time we have to do something right.

The hardest thing we had to come to grips with was that we would never see him again on this earth. Joey is in a better place now, and I was reassured one more time today. Our little granddaughter, Rebecca Grace Nickel, is 20 months old and just beginning to speak. We have pictures in our living room of our other children: Andi, our youngest daughter and also a Marine; Joey and Tommy, the oldest brother, a sailor.

Beneath the photos are Joey's two urns. Rebecca went up and pointed to Joey's picture and said, "Joey," then placed her hand on the urn. She never knew Uncle Joey, and he never saw her, but she could see him. The miracle of a child seeing what we cannot see is a blessing. We will meet once again when we pass, and there will be a new heaven and a new earth.

The trail of ashes started in Afghanistan when the helo went down. Joey's ashes originated there. Most people really don't want to realize what happens in a war. Soldiers die. And when it is your son, your child, the evil of mankind is revealed to you.

The realization struck me that even after our boys were recovered and brought back, a part of Joey and the crew would forever be left behind in that foreign place. These brave men will always be joined in life and in death. The depth of their connection was beyond comprehension. Only the few who were there and stood there after the battle could feel the emotion and pain. This grief is passed on to the families and loved ones of a fallen hero.

Through the many people that we have met since Joey's death, one man stands out far above all others. His name is Sargeant Troy Hayes. He was the army medic who was the first man on the scene to approach the crash site and see our fallen heroes. I truly believe that God brings people together to strengthen us in times like this.

A TV interview I did brought this great man into our life. Somehow, somewhere, he saw it on the national news and contacted me. *What are the chances of that happening?* What an amazing gift from God to speak to him.

Troy Hayes related what he saw and what he did as he approached the wreckage. He said that when he looked at our son, Joey was still locked onto his machine gun. What an amazing kid, ready to fight for this country in the last moments of his life. Sgt. Hayes said all he could do was pray over Joey and ask that he had found peace. Such a man to deliver this message to me.

Our two-hour phone conversation was far from sufficient. The feelings and emotions between two men, one a soldier and one a father, were beyond explanation. In his parting words, Sgt. Hayes said, "I would like to send you a photo taken that morning after the crash." He wanted to put a face on what happened so I would know how much he cared. "If you look over my left shoulder in the picture, the site is about a quarter of a mile back there," he added.

Within seconds of us ending our conversation, the photo appeared on my email. It was the Sargeant, holding an American flag with arms spread out, standing in the desert. I could almost see Joey standing next to him, saying, "Thank you for all the others you have saved." Someday soon, I will meet this extraordinary man, and we will talk more about it.

After recovering our Marines from the site and completing the investigation, they were supposed to send all the remains home to their final resting places. *It didn't quite happen that way.*

They flew all the families to Dover, Delaware, to the Air Force Base, which serves as the reception place for all soldiers killed in any war. We waited there *three days* for our son to return to American soil. The waiting and grief were utterly grueling. We had just spoken to Joey the very same day that he died. The disbelief and pain blurred together.

The six families would meet for the first time under these conditions. As we talked to the other families and learned more about each other, we formed a bond and a love that will never be broken. Listening to some stories that were told and remembering what Joey had told us about his crew made us understand what it took to be a Marine. They were outstanding men, and the love they had for one another really showed through. *Remember them as they were and cherish all that you had with them.*

Everyone at Dover treated us respectfully and kindly. The staff has done this honorable task tens of thousands of times. All the families had to attend a briefing with the mortuary director, who had the grim task of telling us about our sons. To put this as gently as possible, it was stated that we would not be receiving our *entire* son; we would receive additional remains after they were identified. We paused for a moment, but we had already grasped this truth.

War is terrible. Why were we fighting this one? The decision was made to cremate his remains. There were a lot of questions and decisions to be made, and none of them were easy. After all of this, we waited for the airplane to arrive, carrying 19 men who lost their lives. We were not ready for that.

Three days passed, and finally, the families received word that the plane had left Germany. Thoughts consumed every waking moment, leaving no sleep or rest. As more information came in regarding the time of arrival, the feelings became more intense. This would truly be the final realization that they were gone.

We gathered, and our chaplain, Lt. Commander Charles Rowley, prayed with us. While being escorted to the flight line, all I could think was, *"Why?"*

Nothing could change this moment. The icy wind in Delaware was unforgiving, reaching deep into our souls. We just stood there and shivered for what felt like forever. It didn't even seem real; the hazy, cold night was like nothing one could imagine. It was like waking up from a terrible dream, shivering from a cold sweat.

The plane seemed enormous as it landed in the dark at 4 AM. The lights illuminated the tarmac, intensifying the rain and sleet that pelted our miserable heads. All who were present were numb, knowing that these brave

American heroes were about to return to the United States. But there would be no cheering or bands playing music to greet them.

The "Dignified Transfer" is the title given to this honorable ceremony. I shook my head and looked over at Debi. We were both crying. The Marines and Army soldiers who performed the transfer were so solemn and defined in their movements. The way they demonstrated respect and dignity was so powerful that it nearly stopped my heart as they carried their comrades.

The Friends of the Fallen and assigned military personnel consoled the families. The shock and grief were beyond comprehension. I could only imagine the compassion and love these wonderful people have within them to do this job every day. There are great Americans who love this country and will serve no matter what it takes.

By the time we all got back to the hotel, it was breaking daylight. The staff had already made coffee and hot cocoa to warm our souls. Sleep was not part of the program, and the place came alive with people everywhere trying to help. Food was provided, so we sat down and were served graciously by the staff. Their smiles helped wipe away some of our tears.

After the meal, we were feeling the toll of all that had transpired. We couldn't do anything else, and the emotion of helplessness set in. Our scheduled departure was on an evening flight. So, after talking to the other families, we went back to our room to get some sleep. It felt like only moments after I hit the pillow that it was time to head for the airport.

Our CACO Officer (Casualty Officer) attended to every detail, so all we had to do was be there. Without him, this drama would have been unbearable. *Thank you, SSgt. Snoth, you will forever be with us.* The numbness was overpowering, and most of what happened was a vague blur that I wished had never happened. We bid farewell to everyone we could, including those special individuals who left a lasting impact on our lives.

Two such kind souls were Karen Mordus and Charles Rowley. Both have the hearts of saints, and I will always be grateful for their compassion and love. We keep in touch, and someday, we will meet again and visit. Our first meeting was with Karen, and from that moment on, an unbreakable bond was established. Her first words were, "Joey is a Hero." We had multiple conversations, and her presence had a reassuring effect.

Charles "Chuck" Rowley was the head chaplain at Dover. His responsibilities were unbelievable. While at Dover, Chaplain Rowley attended and performed the Dignified Transfers of over 600 Marines. What a toll this must have taken on him. He is now at Camp Pendleton as the spiritual advisor for our Marines and Navy. *Thank you, sir, for your service.*

On the plane ride home, thoughts of the future consumed me. We were aware that it would take a week for Joey to return home and be laid to rest. All this young man had gone through—and for his life to end like this. What would he have become if only he had come home alive?

We received news that he would be sent back on January 30, and the Marine Corps was handling all the arrangements. We owe them a great deal concerning the dedication and honor provided in all aspects of Joey's return home. Joey knew the risks he took and was fully aware of the danger involved in every mission he went on.

None of us are promised anything when we are brought into this world. Joey lived his life with reckless abandonment and with no regrets. He stepped forward when others would not. The 1% makes this country the greatest nation on earth, and we must never forget our fallen heroes.

Joey arrived home by private jet and was escorted by Steve Cassman, his best friend and a fellow Marine. These two men grew up together, and the things they got into still cannot be told. I can only imagine what memories went through Steve's mind on the long trip alone with Joey. They laughed, partied, fought, and did some outrageous things together like brothers would do. These boys always kept their parents worried and guessing about what they would do next. To see the boys grow up and mature into fine, young men made us all so proud.

As the plane neared, all air traffic in Houston was redirected to honor Joey's return. When we looked up, we could see it circle the landing strip, making ready for the landing. It appeared to just float in the sky as if an escort of angels was holding it up there. When the plane touched down, two fire trucks positioned themselves on either side and sprayed an arch of water as it passed under. It was an exceptional sight to behold, with the compassion, consideration, and love of the people who put this salute together. They will always be remembered. *I wish I could thank everyone who helped us during our darkest days.*

As the plane maneuvered into position, hundreds of military members, police, friends, and family stood at attention. This was an unforgettable experience because of the incredible support shown by thousands of citizens, demonstrating the country's care. To see them stop for a moment in their lives and honor what this young man did for them was remarkable.

After the ceremony at the airport, Joey was escorted by a motorcade that had to be seen to really understand the magnitude of what was transpiring. This part of our life was a blur, and only months after were we able to fully appreciate the compassion and respect that was presented on that day. It continues to this day.

The procession traveled 57 miles from Bush Intercontinental Airport, down the beltway, up Interstate-45, past our home, and finally to the funeral home. I made a special request to Mr. Guy Lock, our director for Joey, to pass by his home one more time. Thousands of people lined up the entire route. When we turned onto Dairyland Rd. and down Midway Drive, hundreds of our friends and neighbors were all there.

The roar of over 300 motorcycles that rumbled down the quiet country road announced Joey's *last* journey home. This was not like his *first* homecoming after the prior deployment when I had picked him up at the same airport and driven him to the house. On that visit, we talked, laughed, and grabbed lunch before turning into the driveway.

For his first homecoming, I had made a banner in his honor, which stretched across the driveway. It read, "Welcome Home, Lance Corporal Joey Logan." The expression on his face was priceless, with that huge smile that could light up a room. I had a tear of joy seeing him home, safe and sound. We still have this banner rolled up in my office, but it will never be displayed again.

The final homecoming was so sad, and emotions ran all over the map. All the good memories flashed by so quickly. As the funeral car paused in front of the house, I just wanted to get out and tell him, "Welcome home" once again.

But I knew he was already home. The faces of the individuals I observed throughout this adventure were all identical. I closed my eyes, hoping and praying this was not happening. This street would never be the same. To this day, I still fly both the Marine and American flags out front to remind everyone of his sacrifice.

After we left the house, it was only a short trip to the funeral home, where he would rest for two days. Friends and strangers came by to pay their last respects and to try to comfort us. The true extent of Joey's friends only became apparent to me when they all showed up and I was introduced to each one.

To say this kid got around is an understatement. Most of them knew me very well, mostly because of my reputation as Joey's dad, the mean old cop, and they thought, *Don't mess with him.* Fear is a good thing when kids are growing up; it keeps them guessing. I was so pleased to see old friends that I had lost touch with, some of them over thirty years ago. Age changes all of us, and some I didn't even recognize. I thanked them all for remembering, and I will never forget all who passed by.

I was most impressed by the Marines that stood guard over Joey 24 hours a day for three days until his memorial service. What an amazing group of young men who dedicated their lives to serve and protect this country and each other. I was told by a senior NCO that a Marine was with Joey from the day he died until he was put to rest. He was never left alone, *Semper Fi, always loyal, always faithful*, a virtue that is instilled into each and every Marine. We still have true Americans, and these are living proof. Once a Marine, always a Marine!

I have all their names and will write to each man, thanking them for their service. Seeing them in this moment made me realize what Joey had become. The final day came when everyone gathered for Joey's memorial service at the Willis Community Center. The preparations that were made were truly extraordinary. Without the staff, Mr. Lock, our funeral director, and the Marines, we would not have known what to do or where to start. The entire community rallied to assist us. When the motorcade left the funeral home and made its way to the Center, all the streets were lined with respectful people. What had this boy done to merit such a final homecoming? Despite feeling sad, I was still incredibly proud to witness it all.

The escort pulled into the breezeway, and we were brought inside as preparations were made outside to bring Joey in for the ceremony. Over 600 school students were in front of the building, waving American flags. They had closed the schools to honor this young Marine. I wish I could have given each of them a hug. A huge American flag supported by two fire trucks waved near the entrance of the parking lot.

Once inside the building, I was in awe of all the people who were there. It was a sea of faces, all silently waiting for the Marines to bring Joey home. As they rolled in the coffin, everyone stood and bowed their heads. I felt like I was on fire from all the love and emotion that filled the building. We stood there, Debi on my right and Andi on my left, holding hands. The entire family stood in the front row, joined together for this last goodbye.

Lt. Commander Charles Rowley, the Navy Chaplain mentioned previously from Dover Air Force Base, stood up front next to Joey and his photo. As the commander spoke, all I could think was, *"Why did this happen?"*

No one knows their future and how it will all end, but I knew how Joey had lived. He crammed a lifetime of experiences into a short 22 years. His experiences would fill volumes in any "normal" life. He did and accomplished so much—things I never would have thought of doing when I was his age.

He played hard and died hard; that's all we can expect out of life. So many of us just sit idle through our existence without any direction or goals; *he was not like that*. I just wanted one more chance to sit and chat with him and hear his stories. That is a big part of what has compelled me to write his story and piece together the puzzle parts he played.

Lt. Commander Rowley's decision to give Joey's eulogy was an honor that I only appreciated after he explained his journey from Dover to Texas. This man is the head chaplain at Dover, where all Marine and Navy killed in action come for the Dignified Transfer from combat. *Joey was special*, a stellar Marine with a rocketing future, one of many young men who answered the call and challenge to defend our country. He fought to the very end, along with his crewmen, with no reservations about the duty they performed. Commander Rowley told us that it touched his heart to be asked to give Joey his final goodbye on earth.

After Lt. Cmdr. Rowley spoke his God-given words, the entire auditorium stood up and applauded. Steve Cassman, Joey's best friend and someone Joey recruited, spoke about what it meant to know him. The heart-touching words and love these two boys had for each other were evident in everything he said. After Steve finished, Debi and I both went up, embraced him, and thanked him for being Joey's friend.

Once again, everyone stood and clapped, and the entire room seemed to beam with love and honor. I felt Joey was looking down with his trademark big grin. After this intense moment, members of the local Marine Corps League came forward to pay their final respects. These men served our country in several wars, including World War II, Korea, Vietnam, and the current conflicts. I've gotten to know a few of these exceptional men and have become one of them. The brotherhood is on a level few will know or understand.

It was time to send Joey on his way, but you can never say goodbye at a time like this. Everyone stood as the Marine Guard rolled him down the main aisle outside to still more people waiting for the final salute. They gave us red roses to place on his coffin. All the family placed the flowers and touched him one more time. The Marines gave him the 21-gun salute. My heart jumped with each volley they fired. The Honor Guard folded the flag that covered him. The flag was then handed to Debi, and five additional flags were given to his brothers and sisters.

Each time they presented a flag, the saying was repeated: "On behalf of a grateful nation, we give you this flag in memory of your son." Six men went down that day. The numbers two and six have played an unbelievable part in this entire ordeal. I have written about how it has proven to me that God has his hand in everything we do or see.

The bugler played "Taps." The sound of this music was so clear and loud. It was the final tribute to our Marine. Out of the blue, four airplanes flew over the ceremony in the "Missing Man" formation. As the single plane separated from the other three, I stood up and waved goodbye. Everyone looked skyward in awe as the planes faded into the clouds. What an ending to such a day of honor and sorrow. Joey had made his mark in life, and his passing would not be forgotten.

The Marines loaded him into the waiting car as all looked on. A hollow, empty feeling pierced my heart as the car drove away. He was to be cremated the next day, and his ashes would be returned to the family. This started the trail of ashes that would place some of him in a total of six locations that he dearly loved to be.

The Marine Corps provided two beautiful bronze urns that would contain Joey's ashes. The crash was so intense that two urns were necessary. Our CACO officer and Mr. Guy Lock came to the house with the first urn. A month later, we received a call from Dover Air Base telling us a second urn with his additional remains would be sent home to us. A *second* Dignified Transfer was sent from Dover. Gunnery Sgt. Chad Nordberg flew from Dover to Bush Airport, escorting the second urn. They took great care and made thorough preparations for this leg of the journey.

The second bronze urn was identical to the first—brushed bronze metal displaying the Marine Corps logo, the Eagle, the Globe, and the Anchor, which symbolized the commitment all Marines hold sacred. The urn was encased in a beautifully crafted maple box with a polished brass handle and Joey's name, rank, date of birth, and date of his passing. What an honor for this man to finally bring him home. This box occupied a seat next to the Sgt. on the flight. What were the other passengers thinking when they saw a Marine in his Dress Blues escorting our son home? I know I would have been both proud and devastated all at once.

Once the plane landed, Sgt. Nordberg transferred the urn to Sgt. James Willingham to bring it to the house. Sgt. Willingham was also assigned to our family until all aspects of this assignment were completed. He couldn't conceal the somber expression on his face. Debi and I opened the box and placed the second urn next to the first. This is as complete as it would get. We said our goodbyes to the Marine as we watched him drive away. He had seen three tours in this awful war, and this was not a pleasant memory.

The Trail of Ashes Continues

THOUGH JOEY COULD REST, our journey, and his, was far from over. He would be happier if he could be in places he enjoyed. We were aware of his love for Hawaii, and his friends guided us to his favorite spots there.

It was paradise, like being on a vacation that would never end. There were pictures that Mark Stoltenberg had sent us of Joey and his friends in some of the most beautiful places on Earth. Craig and Camile, Mark's parents, had driven nearly 100 miles to bring these photos to us at Joey's viewing. And they knew we needed them the most. What a gesture from part of the Marine family we did not know.

Mark and Joey had become very close friends during the time they served together. How Mark got them to his parents and then to us was amazing! Because he was still in Afghanistan when the pictures were sent. These pictures will be a keepsake forever remembered by our family. It was the only link we had to what really went on during this war.

As you piece a life together, you can only imagine what they went through. The two urns were placed in our living room next to the pictures of all three of our children who were serving in the military. The room had taken on a different atmosphere as you entered. All that was left was a shadow of the gallant, honorable young man whose life had lain before him. Each time I went into our living room, all I could do was cry.

Debi and I had discussed what we should do with Joey's remains. Our daughters, Tricia and Andi, suggested we get urn crystals to hold some of his ashes. Within a short time, five crystals arrived, along with an urn ring for me. I asked who would place his ashes into the vessels. It was proposed that our funeral director might assist us with this.

I certainly did not think I could do this, but this reasoning changed after some thought. *Why not?* I thought. He was our son! But opening the urn and dipping into his ashes was understandably difficult. The love and emotions had me in a state that cannot be explained.

Debi stood by my side as we unscrewed the top to reveal a tightly sealed plastic bag. The seal was removed, and the bag was opened. I was beside myself, looking at what was left of Joey. Five of the crystals were filled with a tiny funnel that came with the kit. They were necklaces that could be worn around their necks near their heart.

I took the ring, unscrewed a small opening, and poured the ashes in. It was complete; each person would have part of Joey to carry with them. Debi, Tricia, Andi, Melisa, Ssgt. Snoth and I had someone we loved with us. My ring was so special because I could hold him in my hand just like when he was a baby. Remember the number six? Here, six people received his ashes.

My ring received a transformation after that. It had come with a black onyx stone on it. But Joey's birthstone was blue sapphire, just like his eyes. Later, we would make a trip to Montana, where Debi and I visited a sapphire mine. We found and dug up two perfect raw stones to set in the ring. An amazing find, or merely another in a series of small, repeated miracles? God had a way of telling us that Joey was all right if we knew how to listen. It still seems that he is not gone, but there are too many reminders to shock you back into reality.

Time went on, and Joey's unit was still in the war. I initially failed to realize that they had another month following the crash. His comrades were contacting me by email and through Facebook like they were already home back at K-Bay Hawaii. Our world had stopped, but the rest of it was going at full force.

These young people became like family to me. These kids really cared for each other, and only the few that were there could really understand. We would meet all of them soon when the Marine Corps invited us to the Red Lions' homecoming and memorial service for the "Fallen Six." What a life-changing experience this would be. One man who had the biggest impact on me was Sgt. Ricky Combs. This excellent Marine, a dear friend of Joey's, contacted us during our family's trip to K-Bay, Hawaii, for the last memorial.

Ironically, these helicopters were 40 years old, and in the last two years, three of them had crashed. One went down in Hawaii on a training mission over the bay. One Marine, the pilot, was killed, and the other crew members were injured. I remember the phone call from Joey when it happened. He asked if I had seen the news about the crash. I confirmed that I had and asked if he was alright.

Joey said, "Yes," but I could tell he was crying. I told him to pray and thank God he was not flying that day. He was so upset because these were his good friends, and nothing I could say would help. Little did we both know that he would lose his life a year later.

Another crash occurred on a hard landing that Joey was involved in a month before he died. His calls were more frequent during this deployment, and one day, it was him on the other end of the line. However, he was not his usual friendly self, where he typically would say, "Hey! Hey, Daddy-O. What's happening?" Generally, he was always happy and upbeat—but this time, he had no life in his voice.

I asked what was wrong, and he said, "We put one down hard this week, and we were grounded pending the investigation."

"Are you alright? Are you hurt? I asked.

Thankfully, he reassured me that he was alright. He explained that a hard landing in the pickup zone caused the front landing gear to buckle. They would have to scrap that bird.

I told him that he only had a month left and there was nothing wrong with turning in your wings and taking it easy until he left. "Joey, you have had enough fighting for one lifetime. Come home safe, kid. You are already a hero! Don't push your luck!" I cautioned.

He said, "Dad, I can't do that. I would be letting the men down." He was just that kind of man, always thinking of others. I think we both knew something was going to happen, and I was hoping and praying that he would come home safe.

One thing that will bother me forever is why, knowing the record and the problems with these aircraft, the military continued to put our men in harm's way. There was a reason for this being the unit's sundown mission. Why not admit that a 40-year-old machine had no business flying? It belonged in a museum, not in combat!

There will be answers to this someday. Six men died for no reason. Is that war so important? No war has ever done any good. I could go on and on, but nothing will bring them back. There is evil in the world, but there is no helping the Afghan people. War is a way of life for them. It's too late for the Fallen Six, but the rest of our kids need to come home.

Debi and I decided to take two vials of his ashes to spread in Hawaii. One would be sprinkled into Kaneohe Bay off the flight line; the other would be poured into the pool of water beneath Maunawli Falls. The ceremony at K-Bay was another somber reminder that our boys were gone. The presence of all those Marines was an awe-inspiring sight. However, looking through the crowd there, all I could hope was to see Joey step forward and give us a big smile and hug. Meeting all of his friends left a lasting impact on me that will never fade. The warmth and compassion they possessed were nothing but stunning.

Each Marine was honored by their friends and supervisors with a eulogy that showed how close they all were. I remember listening to all of them, but the tears and ocean breeze from the bay numbed my senses. After the official ceremony, it was announced that Mrs. Jennie Riddick, Debi, and I would place their ashes near the flight line into the waters of the bay.

Jennie went first, pouring all of Travis Riddick's ashes into the water. The Riddicks lived in Hawaii and had spent most of Travis's 21-year career there. Tears flowed as his ashes drifted into the blue water.

Now, it was our turn. Debi opened the vial and poured some of Joey's ashes into the bay. As his ashes settled into the clear water, I remembered how the ashes shimmered on the water, just like Joey's eyes did when he was joyful. He was truly happy there. A part of him would always be there, watching the helos fly by.

We went inside, and there was a reception for all the families and the Marines. I met every one of them and had the opportunity to present them with a plaque I had made to honor the Fallen Six. It was given to the unit and now hangs at headquarters in California, where the new unit was formed. Later in the book, I'll talk more about the plaque because it deserves a better explanation and description. One must really appreciate what it means to me and the Marines who served with these great men.

We met Ricky Combs at the reception. He would lead us on the path to the falls and share stories of Joey's barefoot 12-mile hike along this beautiful jungle trail. Remember how everything happens for a reason and how people are joined together? This is another miracle of "twos" that stunned both of us.

After we had spoken for a bit, Ricky said he'd call us tomorrow morning to arrange our hike. Sure enough, my phone rang the following day, and I recognized something familiar about the phone number I was viewing. The last four numbers were "2-9-7-6." In Texas, the last four digits on our home phone were "2-9-7-6." Essentially, Ricky and I shared a similar phone number, but on opposite sides of the world! Ricky didn't know what to say. I let him know Joey had a reason for connecting us and that I appreciated it.

I said, "If you want, call the number, and you'll get our voicemail!"

He said, "I believe you!"

What a way to start a journey! Ricky visited our base hotel the following morning. A group of four, including myself, would hike to Maunawili Falls, a favorite spot for Joey and his friends with a refreshing waterfall cascade. I only discovered this stunning secret location through a photograph sent by Mark Stoltenberg. In the photo, Joey was standing waist-deep in the pool beneath the falls, and of course, he had that huge grin on his face.

I learned later that he'd leaped 40 feet from a high ledge above the pool. It's no surprise he was smiling; he constantly sought excitement, thrills, and challenges. That kid had no fear.

The trail to the Falls had a rich history, starting back with the native Hawaiians who traveled the path barefoot through the jungle. On the outing when the photo was taken, you guessed it; Joey decided to hike the trail barefoot. Joey left his shoes in the truck and ventured out into the jungle with his feet on the ground. As it turned out, the hike turned into a 12-mile trip. Someone in the group had advised that the trail would come out on another mountain where a great Hawaiian battle took place.

Four Marines were on this little walk: Joey, Ricky, Mark, and Joaquin Recuero. They made it to the other mountain. However, I was told that Joey definitely regretted not wearing his shoes on that trek. This was not a walk on the beach; it was some of the most rugged terrain the jungle could provide. But pushing the limits and enjoying life is what Joey was all about. So, knowing this made my trip to the falls even more special.

Today, it was our turn to take the short tour. We parked the cars at the trail entrance and started down the path. The trail was worn down from a lot of foot traffic. I asked Ricky how far it was to the falls.

He said, "About 2 miles."

I looked at Debi and asked if she was ready. She said, "If Joey could do it barefoot, I can do it with no problem."

I thought to myself, *Yeah, sure; I've heard that before!* Ricky and I exchanged a glance and laughed. Off the four of us went, with Ricky leading the way. The trail was steep and winding, following the jungle stream that came from the base of the falls. The lush vegetation and bamboo made it look like a fantasy playing out in front of us.

The falls distracted us from our original purpose. It was up one steep hill and down the other. We stopped for the girls; Andi, our other Marine, was assigned to assist her mom and ensure she made it. Naturally, Debi had worn her flip-flops, which was almost like walking barefoot.

The trail was muddy in some spots, and there were several stream crossings. I got a kick out of the sounds I heard from the rear. Sounds of "ooh," "yuck," "gross," and "wait up" echoed through the jungle. Part of the journey involved rescuing someone out of the mud and finding a lost shoe!

Parts of the trail were built up with timbers so that walking down the steep inclines and declines would be easier. During the several pauses, Ricky and I sat and talked as we waited for the girls. I learned he had lost both his mother and father and really understood what we were experiencing. He said Joey was a brother to him, a reliable source of support when things got rough. He added that Joey was fun to be around; you were always laughing, either with or at him. That is what Ricky would miss the most.

As we meandered along the trail, I could picture the group of young Marines talking their usual trash to each other. It was one insult after another; that's just how they dealt with each other. Being around them was very entertaining.

As we got closer to the waterfall and the emerald pool beneath, you could hear the water rushing over the cliff in the distance. Together, we made our final push toward this special destination. All at once, we were there. I know now what draws people to places like this. It was nature at its best. It was so peaceful and so powerful. There must have been thousands of people who visited this spot, but now it was a place that we knew Joey had visited and enjoyed. The photo was proof enough that he bonded with the water, and here is where we would spread a tiny part of him.

With a vial containing his ashes, Debi planned to swim to the middle of the pool and scatter them in the water. Andi and I stood in the shallow water at the tail end of the pool as Debi swam away from us. Ricky would climb up to the cliff over the pool and wait there so we could have time alone as a family to say goodbye. I could only imagine what was going through his mind as he went around the bend. He'd just returned from a war they'd both fought in. Ricky came home to his wife and little girl, but Joey did not.

We watched as Debi opened the vial and poured the ashes into the water. I wondered if anyone else had ever done this here. As the events unfolded before us, she swam back to the large rock where we were seated. Tears flowed just like the water beneath our feet. Ricky appeared again, as if he had been watching the entire time. The four of us gathered together, and no words were uttered.

Finally, I said, "We need to get back, but first, we need to take some pictures to capture this event in our lives." These pictures would be placed next to the photo of Joey standing in the pool. The hike back went by quietly, and we returned quicker than we had walked out there. Another part of the journey was complete. A power far exceeding our own had orchestrated these events. I am thankful for the hand of God allowing us this privilege.

The Trail Leads to Montana

MONTANA. What can be said about this place—Joey's dream—a piece of heaven? Joey was absolutely in love with this state. His passion for the outdoors drew him to the natural wonder and beauty that surrounds you there. I first took him there on our three-and-a-half-month fishing trip the summer before he went into the Marines. We fished every state west of the Mississippi that had trout in it.

What an adventure for a 19-year-old and his dad. Who really enjoyed this trip the most? This state still maintains its frontier status and has some of the last existing wilderness areas in the lower 48. It is a remarkable place.

I remember watching Joey enjoy fishing in some of the most pristine and breathtaking scenery the eye could behold. He always had a smile on his face and that twinkle in his eye. Catching a fish was just an added bonus. There was one place that made me laugh at Joey. We went into a local fly shop and asked where there was a spot that was remote and held a lot of fish.

The man working there directed us to a map and showed us how to get in there. The road was a rough two-track that crossed a small stream. We parked on this side of the stream. Next to the road was a sign reading, "Know your bears," with a picture of a grizzly and black bear on it. I could tell Joey was wondering as he looked at me.

We grabbed our fishing gear and went off to find the stream. The forest was extremely dense and dark. There were several downed trees that we had to climb over to get through the woods. Anxiety was building as Joey scanned the dark forest.

I asked him, "What's the matter?"

He replied, "Do you really want to fish here?"

I asked why. He said, "The bears! It's spring, and they're in here!"

"Are you afraid of a little old bear?" I asked

He said, "Yep! Let's get out of here!" He looked like an Olympic athlete jumping over hurdles on the way out. I laughed so hard I cried!

Joey and I had many conversations as we traveled 16,000 miles on our fishing trip. And the topic of Montana would come up more and more. One day, Joey told me, "When I get out of the service, I want to live in Montana."

"Me, too," I told him.

"We need to buy some property up here and build a cabin."

"That would be great," I replied.

Joey had already decided where he wanted to be. We came home, and off he went into the Marines. Three short years later, his dream came true. But he was not here.

I hadn't grasped how deeply he longed for this dream to come true. There were two reasons Joey had volunteered for his second deployment. He traded places with another Marine who had a wife and two small children. He told him, "You don't have to go; I'll take your place." Did he save this man's life and lose his? We will never know.

The second reason was so that he could earn more money on deployment to save for his Montana property. When he set his mind on something, there was no stopping him. Time went by, and we received several phone calls from Joey, and the conversation always came back to Montana. Even now, this project is going to happen, and there is a greater guiding force behind it.

On the day that Joey left us, I thought all of my dreams had vanished. The will to go on was gone for me. Debi had faith in his dream, and she talked to me about it one day. She said that Joey wanted to be there and worked so hard for it. I told her that I couldn't go back there and relive those memories.

Debi told me, "You know we have to go back to Montana and show me all the places you two went. This will help me understand the bond of a father and son." I battled with this thought, and I knew she was right; she always is.

One day, I got out the map of Montana, and we looked it over. I showed her places, streams, lakes, and sights that we had seen. She said, "Find a realtor. We are going up there!"

My head was spinning with memories. Could I go back there and retrace our journey? If I didn't, his dream would be lost forever. After some research, I found an area that looked promising. I called an agent in the Helena region, and off we went in our little Toyota. I wanted to take the truck, but the boss reminded me about "gas mileage!" I had to agree, but I cautioned her about the mountain roads and muddy conditions. That went over her head.

We took our time on the way up and navigated a course that would take us to several places Joey and I had visited. One of the most important and breathtaking was Mt. Rushmore and the Crazy Horse Project in South Dakota. Debi and I walked the Mt. Rushmore Monument and were in awe of its grandeur. We felt like the Rocky Mountain Billy goats climbing the cliffs.

Just as we were returning to the car, a double rainbow appeared over the valley below. Rainbows were one of Joey's favorite wonders of nature. Debi said, "He's here watching over our journey," I had to agree.

I explained to her that next, we were going to the Crazy Horse Monument, where Joey first took a helicopter ride. I believe this set in motion his future as an aerial observer in the Marines. Here's a funny story about this ride:

Joey and I had just finished the tour of both sites and on the way, I saw the helicopter rides on the side of the highway. I thought to myself, *wouldn't it be great if we could fly over the entire area and get nose-to-nose with the presidents and Chief Crazy Horse?*

On the way back, we had to go right past the place. I looked over at Joey and said, "How would you like to fly today?"

He said, "What do you mean?"

"Look at the helicopter over there."

He said, "For real?!" and within minutes, we were standing next to the bird. It was a three-seater, one pilot and two passengers.

The following statement was outrageous. Joey said, "Can I sit in the middle?" I asked why. He responded, saying, "Did you see the wire and duct tape on the door hinge?"

I just laughed and insisted he get in! Off we went, flying over some of the most rugged and majestic scenery around, created by nature and man. I could see the ear-to-ear smile on his face, along with a bit of apprehension, as he eyed the door next to me.

We buzzed the granite sculptures and flew directly in front of them. They were impressive, to say the least. Crazy Horse was gigantic, at least three times larger than Rushmore. The pilot, who was an older gentleman, talked to us through his microphone and headsets. He told us about the area and asked if we wanted to see some buffalo.

"Sure," I replied. Our pilot swung down into a hidden valley. There they were, animals just like you would have imagined seeing them when the Native Americans hunted them for food. The pilot swooped down on them and started a mini stampede. To see them running and kicking up a cloud of dust was historic.

Little did I know Joey would be hanging out of a helicopter, firing a machine gun, just a few months later. He went from bailing wire and duct tape to a tethered strap holding him in the helicopter and a feeling of no fear. What a man he had become. I will never forget that first ride and what it meant to both of us.

I recalled this story to Debi as we visited the monuments and captured their wonders. Debi said, "Now I'm beginning to understand why you two loved these places so much."

After exploring Mt. Rushmore for over an hour, we made our way back to the parking lot. It was time to go down to the helicopter and spread some of Joey's ashes, which was where it had all started. As we parked the car, I sat there frozen in time, remembering that moment when Joey and I had taken to the air. Tears started running down my face! I glanced over at Debi, who was crying too.

We got out and walked over to the pad. A man was standing in the doorway, watching us. He didn't say anything; he just stood there. I reached into my pocket, pulled the vial of ashes out, and opened the top. I gently poured the remains out into a little pile and replaced it with the same amount of dirt. I mouthed, "I love you, Joey," and put the cap back on the vial.

Debi and I stood there for a moment, held hands and walked back to the car. Each time we spread ashes, the vial would be filled with the soil from that spot. He gave so much, and we took so little each time. Joey had gone back to another place that he loved.

We drove over to Crazy Horse and toured the site, went to the museum, and ate lunch. We would be gone a month searching for Joey's final resting place and retracing the steps of our adventure. The next chapter in our journey would be meeting with the realtor in Helena, Montana, to see if there was such a place.

We were presented with several land options by our local realtor, Cheryl. We looked at them, but none appealed to us. She did not fully understand what we were going through. We were seeking a remote "off-the-grid" spot where one could get lost in their thoughts. Most of the land was in subdivisions with neighbors and rules. I told her this was not what we had in mind. Some of the areas she presented had access problems with special easements to be secured.

Finally, I told her that we were not interested in these properties. I suggested Debi and I take a break and go to a very special fishing spot that Joey and I loved. She said, "Sure," with a smile of reassurance that we would find the right place.

We headed west towards Philipsburg. I had read that you could mine for sapphires there, so off we went. As I mentioned before, the blue stone was Joey's birthstone, and I wanted to replace the black onyx that was in the urn ring that I wore. The drive there was filled with memories and places from three years ago. We got a motel room for the night, and my dreams were filled with sapphire panning.

By mid-morning the next day, we had arrived at the mine. The employees had all the equipment needed to sift through the piles of dirt and gravel that hid the stones. It was a simple panning operation where you would use a gold pan and water to separate the dirt and rocks. Your search was for a small, unrefined rock that was actually a blue sapphire. Debi and I each sifted through our own piles of dirt.

It was slow going, shoveling enough material into the pan and rinsing it. Once it was cleaned, the larger rocks and debris could be discarded. Picking the sapphires was a difficult task. But once you spotted one, it would sparkle, a bright blue in the sunlight.

Picking them out and placing the stones in a small container made you feel good. We found ten stones that day. What a fun way to spend a day playing in the dirt like a couple of kids. It took our minds off why we were there.

Out of the stones, two of them would fit in the ring perfectly. Another miracle of twos! Those two stones twinkled in the ring, just like his eyes when he had that big grin on his face. What a remembrance, a keepsake forever capturing that glimmer.

Panning and sitting in the sun all day left us exhausted. We traveled west on Hwy 38 to the town of Hamilton and found a place to stay for the night. It was a combination hotel, motel, bar, sky lodge, town meeting place, hangout for all the old retired locals! You name it, this place was it!

Only in Montana could you find such accommodations. It was, of course, a rustic log cabin situated next to a crystal-clear lake. The name of this place was "The Seven Gables." Someday, I need to read the book or watch the old movie with the same name. We settled in for a good night's sleep. I always wake early, and greeting the morning with a Montana sunrise was a magnificent sight. The golden sheen of the sun cresting the mountaintop and bouncing off the lake was breathtaking. I walked up to the water's edge and peered in. You could see trout swimming by, looking for their morning meal.

I went to the restaurant after noticing it was open. This was the same office, bar, and eating place that we had checked into the night before. However, the atmosphere had changed from a beer joint to a morning meeting place for all the locals.

Like the trout, I was pretty hungry. So I sat down at the bar and ordered coffee and breakfast, listening to conversations circulating around the room. Everyone greeted me with a good morning and asked where I was from. I told them that we were from Texas and that we were looking to move to Montana. Everyone in there was retired and had come here to get away from the busy world they had once belonged to.

Our conversations ranged from where to look for land to fishing and restoring old cars. Unlike life in a large city of 4 million, the locals made me feel completely at home. They were all living a simple life without a care in the world. What a great place to start the morning.

Debi had slept in, so I had a good time talking to the old men with their humor and attitudes about life. Two men were particularly entertaining. One man was the perfect example of a mountain man who you would expect to encounter up there. He was a big man, about 6'4", and weighed well over three hundred pounds. He had long hair and a beard, and he wore coveralls.

What really set him off was the eye patch he wore over his left eye. He was very articulate once he began to speak. He got into a conversation with another man, and several one-eyed man jokes were passed back and forth between them. I had not laughed this hard in a while. Once they settled down, I spoke to the other man and learned he was a judge from Missoula, who was staying at his summer home. What a mix of lifestyles and experiences.

That was a delightful time, and I went back to the room to check on the sleepy head, who was up and packing to leave. We went back to the diner so she could eat, and then off we went. Our route was onto Hwy 93 toward Lolo Pass. This was the only pass that allowed you to cross over into Idaho. We stopped at the ranger station so I could show Debi the maps of the area and learn more about the local history and sights to see on the way.

This is the route that Joey and I had taken down along Hwy 12. This road followed the Lochsa River, which Joey loved so much. What an adventure he and I had along this river. The headwaters begin up in the mountain not far from the pass and flow through the Bitterroot Mountains. Joey and I had seen our first wolf on a remote road on our way to a hidden mountain lake. What a sight watching this predator in this pristine wilderness area.

He and I had fished this river for more than a week and covered over 100 miles on the way down to the town of Kooskia. Debi and I would now retrace this journey. I would show her what we saw and had done three years before.

Naturally, I had to fish it, too, as we covered every mile of the river. This place was a wonderful setting to have shared with two people I dearly love: my wife of 35 years and our son of 22 years. Time does change us all, and I wish I could relive those memories.

This river is very special to me. The magnificence of the Bitterroots, where Louis and Clark explored the Clearwater River, can only be explained by visiting. No artist, no writer, can capture the beauty of this region. You have to see it, breathe in the air, and look at every tree to understand what it means to me. If I could picture heaven, this is where I would want to be. I know Joey fishes here regularly with his friends. I can almost see him wading in the water with his fly rod overhead and a cutthroat trout tugging on the line.

This reminds me of another fishing story with Joey. We were on the Locsha around the 30-mile marker on Hwy 12. This road runs along the river, and there are several pull-offs where you can stop and fish. What attracted us to this spot is a giant boulder, about the size of a small house, that sits in the middle of the river. It must have rolled off the mountain centuries ago and come to rest there. I'm sure glad I wasn't there when it came rumbling down and crashed into the river!

There is a beautiful pool that formed after centuries of water cut around it and made a good hiding place for hungry trout.

Joey and I walked down to the bank and began to fish. I hooked into a nice cutthroat trout and released it. Joey inquired about my lure, so I showed him. He went to his tackle bag and tied one on. I suggested he cast to the base of the rock to catch a salmon or bull trout hiding in the deep hole. He let fly with the lure, and it went sailing further than he expected.

You guessed it; he caught the boulder. I could not resist telling him, "You have this entire river to fish, and what do you catch? The biggest rock in it!"

Needless to say, Joey didn't appreciate the comment on his fishing technique. We exchanged a few nasty remarks, and I asked him, "Are you going to swim out there and get my lure?"

He said, "I'll get it loose by just pulling on the line." Well, that lure is still hanging on the rock—four years later. Nice going, Joey!

I took Debi to this spot and told her this story. She laughed, saying, "That's why you are always buying more lures!"

That day, seeing that huge old rock with Debi brought both laughter and tears, recalling memories and grieving the loss of future ones with Joey. As we stood there, I had my fishing rod in my hand with the same lure I used that day. I made a few casts and hooked up with a fine trout. I couldn't help but think, *this one's for you, kid,* as I gently released that fish back into the water.

There was one more place to show Debi on the river. It is the holding pens the Fish and Game Department uses to catch salmon to breed more fish. It is a fascinating place. Thousands of fish are caught in traps set in the river. Through a particular process, the fish are stripped of eggs and milt to produce new fish. These fish are raised there and then taken to Orofino,

Idaho, where they are kept until they reach a specific size. Then, they are released into the river system and return to the sea to mature into salmon.

These same fish returned five years later to the headwaters of the Lochsa to spawn again. The cycle of life goes on all around us, and yet very few see it. Joey and I visited this place, and the wonder in his eyes was amazing. He understood and was in awe of the experience. We all live, and all die, but the time in between should be filled with good things like this.

Debi and I walked a short distance from the hatchery to a little stream, which was the source of the river, high in the mountains. We planned to sprinkle Joey's ashes into the water. We knew he loved this place, and by doing this, he could flow back down to the ocean like the salmon and complete the cycle of life.

I went to the streamside, opened the vial, said a little prayer, and watched as the ashes flowed away. Leaving, we felt assured of Joey's well-being, knowing a part of him would stay there. We decided to go back to Missoula and make one last attempt to find a location to fulfill Joey's dream in Montana. At our hotel, I browsed the yellow pages to find a local realtor who could help us.

It was just like my eyes were drawn to one particular ad, so I called the number. A man answered; his name was Mark Twite. I explained what we were doing and why, and he said without hesitation that he had a couple of places that we would like. Of course, I had heard that before and was not too enthused. He insisted we come by his office to look over the properties, so we did.

After talking to Mark, I noticed that there was something different about him that I liked. We sat there and explained the story of Joey's dream. We reviewed maps and talked about locations, narrowing it down to three locations.

Montana's reality is what I call "self-service." The realtors point you in the right direction and then turn you loose with a guided tour or sightseeing on the way. Mark knew that the maps and GPS would help us locate the places. The high demand for perfect properties and the considerable distances involved make statewide showings of remote locations financially unfeasible for realtors. I fully understood and did not mind a bit.

Actually, it was really enjoyable to explore the area. However, finding those places, especially while driving off-road in a Toyota Corolla in the mountains, was a little unnerving.

On a Side Note: I did most of the driving on the mountain dirt roads and received a lot of driving instructions from my wife throughout the month. She offered statements like, "Slow down. You're getting too close to the edge. You're going to kill us. There's no one around here to help us if we have a wreck," etc. I seriously considered driving off the mountain to end all the constant nagging!

I said, "Do you want to drive? Now, sit there and keep quiet. Joey and I drove over 16,000 miles with no help from you. And we made it back okay, thank you very much." Too much time in a car with your wife is not a good thing. That's why I took up fishing; you can't hear her from the boat. (This phrase is actually printed on a t-shirt Debi gave me!)

We went to the first tract of property that Mark had suggested. It was located 12 miles off the main road and sounded too good to be true. Weather and water often play a big part in getting into some of these places, and this property was no exception. It had just rained, and there was runoff throughout the area.

The property's remoteness became increasingly apparent the further we drove. The people who live out here are a different breed. They are truly like the early pioneers who settled here. We were learning this quickly.

The road wound up the mountain, probably following the same route the early miners took when they were exploring for gold. The road had not improved much since that time. There were mud holes and rocks in the road that had rolled down from the steep banks on both sides. We had often had to get out and move them in order to move ahead.

The only thing that we did not experience was a downed tree across the road, but a chainsaw is a necessity up there. Without one, you might get in but may not get out. Streams were running along the route, which looked like a great place to fish. I even suggested stopping to fish a couple of times on the way up. But the boss said, "No way!" I'll go back there someday without her in a four-wheel-drive truck.

This location seemed like a hundred miles rather than twelve, as Mark's directions had indicated. Debi and I realized that we were not that brave and this may not be the right location. However, the scenery was breathtaking. There was even an old ghost town up there, and I could see why it was abandoned. What a remote place to live.

This was a mining town, and after the gold ran out, so did the people. There were piles and piles of old mining tailings along the road. These are all the rocks and stones left over from the mining. They had been there for over one hundred years. What history lay there? The tons of rock and back-breaking work for a little gold. In my mind, I was already planning my first pan for gold once we got settled up there.

We finally made it to the end of the road, parked the car, and gave a sigh of relief. The only problem was we had to go back the same way we came. The property was absolutely stunning and spanned 440 acres. What a paradise for a real mountain man. You could live back here without a care in the world because the real world does not exist here.

It was so quiet; no man-made noise to clutter up your senses. There are very few places on the planet like this. What a place to sit and dream about the past. But as beautiful as it was, we both realized that this was not the place.

On the way back down, I could feel Joey's dream slipping away. Despite looking for nearly a month, nothing had yet struck us as his final resting place and a new beginning for so many others. It was still early in the day, and there was one tract of land left on our list. Off we went back down the highway toward the last destination, hoping a miracle would occur.

Do you know that feeling when something wonderful is about to happen? A sense of peace came over me with the warmth of the afternoon sun leading us west toward the next property. Looking at the map and description of the land, again, it seemed too good to be true. We would later understand that this was a gift from God, with Joey guiding the way.

As we turned off the main road onto the forestry road, a miracle began to happen. I had almost given up hope, but in the last and final hour, things were looking up. This piece of heaven was 164 acres, completely surrounded by Lolo National Forest. That in itself was totally amazing. This never happens in the real estate market.

Was this an accident or a gift? The drive into the property was so easy I thought I was dreaming. It was only three and one-half miles off the main county road. How could this place be hidden from the world? No one knew it was for sale. It was listed, but it seemed invisible for some reason.

Pulling up to the main gate was something to behold. The entrance was a huge iron pipe swing gate set on a post that blocked the road onto the property. It was painted forest green and had a lock on it. Someone went to great lengths to secure this passage.

The trees on both sides prevented a vehicle from driving around. So we parked the car and walked around this massive piece of iron. The unbelievable part of this place is that all the forestry roads leading here had ended, and there was no further access to the forest beyond this point.

Could this be true? The maps don't lie. This was the drop-off spot for hundreds of square miles of some of the last existing wilderness areas in the lower 48. The miracle was beginning to unfold before our very eyes.

What was making this happen? The answer came clearly. Joey had paid for this piece of heaven on earth with his life. The sacrifice made was the ultimate price one could pay. I was overwhelmed by the pain of *losing* him and *gaining* this place for him.

We both knew, from the beginning, this was meant to be. With tears in our eyes, Debi and I shared a look, confirming this.

She said, "This is the place!"

I replied, "I know."

A sense of joy, sadness, and relief flowed through us as we looked to the west. The sun was moving toward the mountain tops, and evening was upon us. What a scene to behold. The setting of the sun and a new beginning to the future were upon us. There was a peace in these mountains that I had never experienced. It was a sanctuary from the world that had taken our son away. No longer would he have to face the evil that he saw. At last, he would rest.

The Trail to the White River in Arkansas

THIS WOULD BE a short journey compared to our quest for a final resting place in Montana. The river brought back so many memories of the fishing trips Joey and I had taken when he was a teenager. The White River is part of a hydroelectric dam system that provides power to the grid. In doing so, large lakes were formed, which provide water for the turbines that produce electricity. While this is good, it also creates some of the best trout fishing east of the Rockies. The water moves from the bottom of the reservoir and stays at 50 degrees year-round. You don't want to wade out into this water even in July.

The flow of the river is controlled by the amount of water needed to supply power on any given day. It can be a challenging river to fish because of the erratic water flow. One day, it will be slick and calm. Hours later, you will be washed down the river. This makes it interesting if you wade out to a gravel bar and the water comes up, leaving you stranded there until it goes down.

Joey and I would head up to the river every summer and camp out in one of the parks situated along its banks. Catching a trout there is so easy because the State of Arkansas stocks over a million fish in the river annually. This was a great place to take a kid fishing. These trips held the promise of adventure and fishing, which we both eagerly awaited.

You could use all kinds of tackle, but as he progressed, fly-fishing became what appealed to him the most. There's nothing like watching a rainbow trout inhale a dry fly floating along with the current. The flash of the metallic colors, red, green, black, and silver, streaking through the water and trying to control that fish can be a challenge. But watching Joey yell, "I got one; get the net!" was what these trips were all about. There were some huge brown trout that lurked in some of the deep holes and under the cut banks. They would surprise you as they grabbed your lure and took off running down the river.

I remember one morning when a mist was still hanging over the water. It looked like smoke swirling back and forth as the sun crept over the hillside. The scene painted its own picture that will forever be printed in my mind.

Joey put his waders on first, and off he went, disappearing into the mist. I could only see glimpses of him as his fly rod swinging back and forth over his head. The yell, "Fish on! Hurry, it's a big one!" came just as I started putting on my boots.

Net in hand, I raced to the river to where the battle was occurring. What a sight! Joey's fly rod was doubled over, and the big trout was stripping the line. He said, "I can't hold him!"

The excitement was more intense as the fish ran even further downriver. Joey had to wade further along the river bank as the fish had already made up his mind about where he was going. I followed along, giving advice as the battle continued. By this time, the mist had lifted, and we could see the vast swirls the fish made in the water as he powered away from Joey. He looked at me and asked, "What should I do?"

I replied, "Adjust our drag and put a little more pressure on him."

"I don't want to lose him."

This tug of war went on for quite a while. Finally, Joey was gaining line. As the fish neared, we could see the bronze body covered with brilliant red, black, and orange spots. Seeing this fish was breathtaking and something only a fly fisherman can appreciate this vision. Fly-fishing is a quiet sport; it is just you and the fish.

The trout was about to surrender. Joey gently eased his rod upward, and I slipped the net under him. What a beauty! The joyous smile on Joey's face was priceless. He admired his catch and then gently removed the hook. The brown trout measured 28 inches. We gave each other a high five and Joey released the fish back into the river. As we watched the trout slowly swim away, I felt a great pleasure coming over me. It was because of the experience we shared together.

Now, Debi and I were here for the next journey that would allow us to leave a small part of Joey in this beautiful setting. The ride there was full of memories, and as we traveled, I shared several great fishing stories with Debi. I let her know then that I was going to write a book detailing our fishing and hunting excursions. I only wished that there would be more stories to tell. The memories will have to be enough because it's hard to replace a fishing buddy like Joey. Every time I remember those trips, I'm overcome with joy and sadness.

Debi and I had made reservations at Gaston's fishing lodge along the White River. This place had cabins located right on the water. You could see and hear the water from the room. This differed greatly from the tent camping Joey and I did when we visited the area before.

I explained to Debi that there was nothing like camping on the river and having fresh trout for breakfast. But Debi said, "I need a warm bed and steak and eggs in the morning." So, I had to give in to her request on this trip.

After a good night's sleep, I went down to the office and rented a boat for our passage down the river. There was a special place on the river where we would pour his ashes. It was a spot named White Hole and a place of natural wonder. Its name is due to the pool's base being entirely solid white limestone. As you approach it from the rapids from just upstream, the river's standard bed of gravel opens up into stunning white. The white bottom and crystal-clear water create a fishbowl effect, making every fish visible.

The boat was ready for us to float down the river. We took a pleasant ride, allowing the current to take us to our destination. As we traveled, I highlighted some of Joey's and my previous camping and fishing locations with Debi. It was a beautiful morning and naturally I had to bring my fly rod.

Our destination was about seven miles downriver from where we had put in. I waited until we had reached White Hole before I made my first cast. Within minutes, I hooked a nice rainbow trout. The brilliant colors flashed in the gin-clear water. "This one's for you, Joey," I said as Debi applauded.

Wishing Joey could see it, I released the fish I'd caught. I asked Debi if she was ready to sprinkle his ashes into the water. She replied, "What a wonderful place to let him fish forever." As she opened the vial and poured the ashes into the water, I cried uncontrollably.

The tiny particles of his remains once again sparkled as they settled to the bottom. There is something about Joey and water that bond together. I pulled the boat to shore, and we both sat there for a while. It was so peaceful watching the water flow by, daydreaming about the past. It was time to leave this spot and make our way back upriver.

I started the motor and pointed the boat upstream, looking back every once in a while to a placed that meant so much to a dad and his son. For as long as I can, I plan to revisit this fishing spot annually.

Montana—The Sundown Mission

SPRING 2013 found us returning to Montana after a long year and an even longer winter. The Red Lion Project was well underway, and construction of "The Fallen Six" cabins would start soon. The first and most important part of this final journey was to place Joey's headstone and spread his ashes on the land he paid for with his life. Spring in Montana is filled with lots of new growth; regeneration came forward from under the fallen snow. Life was abundant everywhere.

I didn't mind the long trip up here this time. It was filled with a new purpose and excitement that I thought I had lost. This place would become the beginning of many new memories that would help our guests heal from the visible and invisible scars of war. The peacefulness of the mountains is beyond words. Nature has a way of fixing itself, and we do, too. The vision of Joey's dream was coming true.

Who would have known his dream would have taken a turn like this? It had gone from a cabin in the woods where a father and son could enjoy each other's company to a retreat for Marines. The thought of veterans and their families enjoying this dream filled me with joy.

The Sun Down Mission was the end of the Lucky Red Lions, the HMH 363 as a unit. It was decided before they deployed to Afghanistan that the unit would be disbanded and all personnel would be reassigned. Joey and I had a conversation about this shortly before he left. He was a part of a unit that had its beginning in 1952. What a history of brave and gallant men who fought for their country in some of the most intense conflicts we have ever entered into.

It bothered Joey and the Marines he served with to know that one day, they would say, "You don't exist." It was like getting kicked out of the house to never come back again. Did Joey know this would be his Sun Down Mission? Why didn't they decide to disband before this deployment? Would it have mattered if they did not go to fight this unwinnable war? Six great men died for no reason. The cause, the mission, and saving a country were meaningless.

Much preparation went into this trip. Debi and I's primary goal was to set Joey's headstone. This was a private matter between just us. We picked a location in the center of the property. The heart of this land would be his final resting place. The exact spot was in a little meadow surrounded by pine trees. The ground was covered with fresh green grass that had sprouted through the snow only weeks before.

We looked to the west and made sure there was a perfect view of the mountaintops. In this way, Joey could see the sunset each day, just like his Sun Down mission. Together, we sprinkled his ashes on the new growth that was all around us. A new beginning was happening, another miracle for us to cherish.

After his ashes faded into the ground, it was time to place his headstone. I lifted the 130-pound stone from the truck and put it over his ashes. The stone had his name, rank, date of birth, date of passing, a cross, and the Marine Eagle, Globe, and Anchor. This stone was a fitting memorial for such an extraordinary young man. More tears were shed. They will never end. We paused for a moment, looking at the grandeur surrounding us.

This will forever be a sacred place, a tribute to Joey and his fellow Marines. They gave so much and received so little. It was time to move on and work on the future. We posted a marker at the gate that read: In Honor of the Fallen 6, Marine Heavy Helicopter Squadron 363.

The marker listed each man's name, age, and hometown as follows:

Cpl. Joseph D. Logan, 22, Willis, TX
Capt. Daniel B. Bartle, 27, Ferndale, WA
Capt. Nathan R. McHone, 29, Crystal Lake, IL
MSgt. Travis W. Riddick, 40, Centerville, IA
Cpl. Jesse W. Stites, 23, North Beach, MD
Cpl. Kevin J. Reinhard, 25, Colonia, NJ

The Red Lion squadron patch was embossed in red and green on the marker. And the last wording stated: "Semper Fidelis to our Fallen Marine Heroes, WE WILL NEVER FORGET YOU!"

I thought the trail of ashes had ended there on the mountaintop in Montana, but it had not. Shortly after, we received a letter from Dover, Delaware, informing us that there were remains from the crash that could not be identified.

The official statement read: "There will be a Group Burial of the remains from this incident. These are remains that, for whatever reason, could not be attributed to a single member involved. They will be buried in a single casket at Arlington National Cemetery on Thursday, October 24, 2013, at 11:00 hours. All six names will be carved into the headstone, along with the date of the incident.

October 24th also happened to be Debi's birthday. There was another miracle of twos. Rest in final peace, all you great Marines, SEMPER Fi, and God Bless.

In the pages that follow, I will recount some wonderful experiences God gifted me with during the summer before my son deployed. Even though I had no clue back then that his life would be so short, I would never trade that incredible summer of *Fishing with Joey*.

Making Memories with My Son

What moves through us is a silence, a quiet sadness, a longing for one more day, one more word, one more touch. We may not understand why you left this earth so soon or why you left before we were ready to say goodbye. But little by little, we begin to remember not just that you died but that you lived. And that your life gave us memories too beautiful to forget.

Joey Had Balls

THIS STORY IS for our Marines, and it's not what it sounds like. (Or maybe it is!) The story is on par with the constant beer-drinking and eating crayons.

In his senior year of high school, Joey experienced a serious accident. He was horsing around, wrestling with one of his friends, and fell on a broken glass from a table that got knocked over when he slipped. He called me in a panic, saying he had a severe hand injury and blood was spurting out. It would not stop.

Unfortunately, Joey had severed the artery in his wrist. I could not get to him quickly, as he was several miles away. It is such a helpless feeling when your kid is hurt, and you can't help. I advised him to take his belt and wrap it around his wrist as tight as he could. He and his friend applied the tourniquet and stopped the bleeding. The next thing I told him was to have his friends rush him to our local hospital.

In a short time, we were on the way to meet them there. Debi and I arrived at the emergency room and were taken back to Joey's room. The doctors told us that it was very serious and that he would have to be taken to the trauma center in Houston.

I wanted to see the injury, but I wasn't expecting what I saw. Joey's face showed complete despair when he saw the injury. The main artery, tendons, and nerves connecting his wrist to his hand and fingers had been severed.

He will never use that hand again, I thought to myself. They medicated him for the pain, and he was fading in and out. The ambulance loaded him, and we followed behind to Houston, where we went to the Ben Taub Trauma Center, one of the best trauma hospitals in the country.

Joey underwent immediate surgery. We waited and waited, and eight hours later, a doctor came out to tell us he was stable but had done extensive damage to his hand. Our hearts sank. He would spend the next several days in the hospital.

That evening, we asked if we could speak to the doctor who performed the surgery. No one seemed to know who he was, only that he was the surgeon "on call" that night. I told the nurse, "That's impossible. Someone knows the name of the surgeon who performed the operation."

The nurse checked and then told us he had already left. She informed us that Joey's medical records did not list the surgeon's name. All we wanted to do was thank him for saving Joey's life that night. To this day, there is no record of who the doctor was. I had different people check the records during Joey's long physical therapy process. Not one bit of information ever surfaced. Absolutely nothing!

Do you believe in miracles? Or angels sent from heaven? Given everything that had occurred in the past three years, in retrospect, this was Joey's initial encounter with the divine.

Now getting back to Joey having balls: I have to laugh every time I look around at the assortment of balls Joey kept on hand. They are blue, round, hard, and soft. There are many of them, and they all played a significant part in his life.

Two important balls were the pair of exercise balls he used to strengthen his hand following his accident. At first, he had three appointments a week and I would take off work to take him each time. Joey was really depressed, always concerned that he might never gain back full use of his hand. His enlistment in the Marine Corps had already taken place, and he was scheduled to begin basic training in late October 2008, only nine months after the accident in January.

I would go in with him, wait, and ask about his progress. It was slow and painful. His dreams of becoming a Marine were vanishing. Now, I hate to say it, but I wish his hand had not recovered.

FISHING WITH JOEY

Every time Joey finished a session, a wide grin appeared on his face. I asked him why he was so happy. He said, "Did you see that nurse that I'm working with? She's a babe!" Joey was falling in love with his nurse. Well, not really; she was in her late twenties, single, and gorgeous. Joey was eighteen and just happy to be holding hands with her.

One time, I told her, "You and I both know Joey has a crush on you!"

She laughed and said, "I know. Building a rapport with my patients greatly contributes to their healing process from injuries and trauma. We try to form a bond because it makes things work out better. But I'm 28 years old, and he is only 18. So it ain't gonna work out, anyway." This lady really cared, knew her job, and did it well. We would laugh and wave after each session.

As time went by, Joey's progress reached a standstill. There was little improvement. It was now the end of June, and he seemed quite down. He would look at his hand, move his fingers, and a feeling of rage would come over him. I didn't know what to do to help him. Then, one day, I had an idea that would change both of our lives.

I loved fishing, and Joey did, too. We were outside just talking one day, and I asked him if he wanted to go fishing this summer. He shrugged his shoulders and grumbled, "I guess so..."

His life was clearly crumbling before my eyes. I told him to go and get his fly rod out of the garage. He came out with it in his *right* hand instead of his injured *left* hand.

"Grab the rod in your left hand and hold on to it," I said.

"I can't," he replied.

"Yes, you can," I said, "and we are going fishing!"

As he attempted to use his hand, the look I received from him was one of desperation. He had given up. He said, "Where are we going? Arkansas?"

"Maybe we'll start there," I answered.

He just looked at me with a puzzled expression. I had talked to his doctor and therapist, and they both said they had done all they could do for him;

the rest was up to him. But I saw that what he needed was a purpose to continue.

Joey and I spoke again about fishing over the next few days. I knew if I did not do something with him, he would get worse. I talked to Debi about what I was going to do. The plan I hatched was simply to go to work, tell them I was retiring, and go fishing for the rest of my life.

The people at work looked at me like I was crazy! Well, maybe so, but after 28 years of being a cop, I'd had enough. It took me a day and a half to turn in my paperwork, and suddenly, I was a free man.

I came home with a new outlook on life. The next thing I did was to take Joey to get his passport. He asked why he needed a passport, to which I replied that since he was going into the military, it would be good if he got one. In a short time, he obtained it and tucked it away. It was time to make a few plans!

Over the years, we had gone fishing in several places, either with the entire family or just him and me. Joey was the only one out of five kids who really enjoyed the outdoors, especially fishing. I had subscribed to several trout fishing magazines over the years, and those became my source of information for most of our fishing trips. Looking back, for some reason, I kept all the magazines and maps, highlighting each article and the places that we were to visit on our fishing trip together. I didn't expect this to be our final fishing trip, but it turned out to be the ultimate one.

It took us a few days to pack everything we needed for the trip. The truck was stuffed with all the gear needed for our expedition to every trout stream across the continent imaginable. I was so excited knowing what I had planned for him, and he had no clue what was in store!

We said goodbye to Debi, pulled out of the driveway, and headed north. We were going on a trip that would shape a young man's life and miraculously heal a damaged hand. Fishing with Joey will be a full-length book telling huge fish tales and the bond of love and friendship between a father and son.

Arkansas: White River Fishing Trip

THE WHITE RIVER was the first stop on our fishing trip of a lifetime. I had an idea that would distract Joey from his injured hand, and it worked. After six months of physical therapy, it seemed like he hit a stone wall. His depression deepened, and the only cure was to go fishing. I discussed my idea with Debi, and she said without hesitation, "Go!"

I approached Joey with a proposition that was really very simple. I asked him to go and get his fly rod and bring it outside to try something. He came walking out of the garage with the rod in two pieces. "Put it together and grab hold of it," I said.

"I can't!" he responded.

"Try it," I told him.

He was starting to give me a little attitude, so I adjusted my plan by saying, "I'm going trout fishing, and if you want to stay home, don't put that pole in your hand."

I could see him looking at the scar on his hand and wrist as he squeezed the cork handle. "Now go get all the fishing gear, tent, and camping equipment and start loading the truck," I said.

"What do you want me to bring?" he replied.

I told him to bring everything we needed to catch trout. Joey looked puzzled, but he went about hauling stuff out onto the driveway for me to look at. It took us the remainder of the day to sort out gear and decide what to take on our fishing excursion.

Joey said, "Don't you think this is a lot of stuff?"

I replied, "Not really!" Now I could see the wheels turning in his head as he thought, *What is Dad up to now?* Little did he know we were about to embark on an exciting trip and adventure!

My plan was to go on the fishing trip of a lifetime, visiting all states west of the Mississippi with trout fishing. Given Joey's situation, what could be better than fishing and enjoying nature with a kid who loves it? Debi and I planned out the details. We observed how Joey was doing; a trip like this could only improve his attitude.

He had already enlisted in the Marines and was going to report in October. But with his hand like it was, his dreams of becoming a Marine were all but lost. I contacted his recruiter in Conroe and promised that he would be ready by the time we came back. Looking back, I know this trip was meant to be. We all have an appointed time on this earth, and I'm grateful for the time we spent together.

Months before this trip, I had already planned the route we would be taking. I read every article in the magazines *American Angler*, *Fly Fishing*, and *Fly Fisherman*, along with fish and game books from all the states and provinces where we would fish. I made detailed notes about the specific locations of trout in streams, rivers, and lakes across all states. What a notebook that became!

Looking back, I'm glad I did. It helped me recall every step in this incredible journey. America is a great country to fish in, and many of the places are incredible, not just for the fishing but also for the scenery and people you meet along the way.

We loaded the truck loaded with a ton of gear. And believe me, we used all of it during our trip and then some. That's the great thing about having an understanding wife who is also a loving mother. Not all women would let two crazy men take off to parts unknown for three and a half months to go fishing!

Both the truck and my desire to spend time with a cherished kid were overflowing. Joey was the youngest of three boys, and after all the stunts his two older brothers pulled growing up, I figured the safest place for this one was with Dad. We backed out of the driveway and waved goodbye to Mom. The first thing Joey asked was, "Where are we going?" I told him we were headed to Arkansas.

"That figures," he said. "It's the first place I ever caught a rainbow trout." Off we went up Highway 59 and headed to the White River located below Bull Shoals Lake. We were on our way to an amazing fishing spot!

Arkansas Fish and Game stocks over a million trout in this river each year. Even a blind hog could find an acorn here in the fishing sense of the word. It took us most of the day to drive up there, and we planned to camp at the state park close to Bull Shoals Dam.

We arrived at the campsite, unloaded, and set up our tent. By the time we settled in, the only thing we could do before dark was to get our fishing licenses. Oh, I forgot to mention that we had our canoe strapped to the truck's camper. This would enable us to fish in many different places and explore as we paddled along.

There's something about camping along a river: hearing the water rush by, smelling the moist air as the night breezes flow through the tent, and, most of all, experiencing the peace it gives you. Lying there, thinking how lucky we were to be able to spend time together, helped us fall asleep with dreams of big trout at our doorstep. Morning came early, and I started brewing some coffee while Joey continued to sleep. However, the smell of fresh brew got him up and ready for the day.

The setting was the rugged Arkansas Ozark Mountains, with the White River nestled between the rugged rock faces and mixed forest trees. This was a special morning because a thick fog lay on the river like a ribbon winding along its course. As we looked out over the river, I cooked some bacon, eggs, and toast for breakfast. We were both anxious to get in the water, so the meal was quick.

Our fly rods were outfitted with a double nymph setup, one with a gold bead head and the other with silver. Above that, on the tapered leader, was a small strike indicator set at about three feet in depth. This method gives a fish a first and second look as it passes by. It's quite an ordeal putting on your waders and fly vest, which is filled with all that is needed: a net, polarized sunglasses, and a hat.

I read the water, looking at the flow, and told Joey to wade out about waist-deep so his cast would reach the deep hole along the opposite bank. The fog made it difficult to see him in the river as he cast the flies upstream from the pool. There had to be a hungry trout waiting for a meal to pass by. I stood on the bank, watching what almost looked like a ghostly figure moving in and out of the mist. I could hear the whipping sound of the fly line as it cut through the air on its way to the perfect spot. I often replay this moment over and over in my mind, wishing for one more cast with him.

Suddenly, the peaceful silence was interrupted by the well-known cry of "Fish on! Get the net!" The sound of Joey's voice told me he had a good one; the fish was stripping line, and I could hear the clicker screaming away as the trout made a run downstream. There was a lot of splashing going on, and as I waded closer, I could see his rod bent over almost doubled.

"Hurry up and get over here; I can't net this one myself," Joey yelled.

I saw the swirls and ripples the trout was making several yards downstream. "Go with him down the river until you can turn him," I yelled.

There we were, side by side, fighting a battle with a trophy trout. Being there was like a dream come true! The tug of war continued between the fish and the fisherman. Joey would gain some line, and the trout had other ideas with strong head shakes and short, powerful runs along the rocky bottom. I was hoping it would not break the leader line.

Joey said it felt like a brown trout, the way it was pulling and staying close to the bottom. Browns have that characteristic, and once you've hooked a few, you know what's on the other end of the line. I could see the excitement and anxiety building as the fish turned its head and started responding to the force of the rod pulling it closer.

I stood ready with the net, but the fight was not over yet. The water was gin clear, and I saw the flashing color of the bronze back and the leopard-like dark brown and red spots on its side. The sun was up above the ridges now, and it showed down into the water that once was gray and foggy. The setting came alive with brilliant metallic flashes as the trout spun around to make another short run.

Joey started backing up into shallower water as the fish rolled and grew tired from the fight. We could see the large, hooked jaw and girth of the fish. It was a big male, and I could see the tiny fly lodged in the corner of its mouth.

How a tiny hook like that can hold a fish like this still amazes me! We worked in tandem as the trout was pulled closer to the net. I had it ready—wet and in the water—so the fish would not respond to any sudden movement or splashing. "Don't miss it," Joey remarked. I reminded him that this wasn't my first rodeo!

With a gentle sweet of the net, the trout was lifted out of the river. The smile on Joey's face and the gleam in his eye were priceless. We exchanged a high-five and admired this beautiful creature. Joey reached down with his forceps and gently popped the hook from its mouth. "That's the best trout of my life; get a few pictures of it before I release it back."

The trout was lying in the net, and it measured 25 inches long! Not bad for a brown. Joey knelt in the water next to his trophy while I snapped a few pictures. "Time to turn him loose and let him fight another battle," Joey said.

The mighty trout slid from the net and slowly tailed into deeper water. Returning what nature gives is essential to sustain the cycle of life. We gave each other another high five and sat on the riverbank, savoring the moment.

It was still early morning, and there were several rainbow trout that would take a fly. We had this stretch of the river to ourselves. During the week, there aren't many people on the river. On almost every other cast, a trout would grab the tiny fly and perform its dance underwater. "Rainbows" are exactly as their name implies: metallic speedsters. They often leap out of the water, trying to throw the hook. Their vibrant colors, including a crimson streak along their body and a speckled green back with a silver underside, make them truly spectacular.

This river had a limit of ten rainbow trout per person per day, so most of the time, we practiced catch-and-release. On this day, we kept two fish each for dinner. There was a great little restaurant nearby that would cook your catch of the day. We ate there a few times on earlier trips.

After spending the whole day on the water, the side dishes make for a massive meal. You even got a choice of how you wanted the fish cooked: fried or spicy-breaded. After a meal like that and a "to-go" box to boot, we headed back to our camp on the river. The evening in early June was pleasant and calm near the water. We started a campfire and sat around talking about what we were going to do in the morning.

Remember the canoe we had brought along? A man named John from the area would pick us up downstream, around twenty miles away from our camp. We would start out first thing in the morning. This river is regulated by the Bull Shoals Dam, a hydroelectric power plant. The turbines are activated when there is a need for power in the grid.

Early morning is the best time to put in and get ahead of the water surge moving downstream. So, we were up and ready by 7:00 a.m. and in the water, paddling down the river. Once midstream, the current would move us along at a gentle pace. I sat in the rear and did the steering to move the canoe into the right places that held the most trout. The water was so clear you could see almost every stone, submerged log, and structure to cast your fly.

I fished a little and mostly enjoyed the river and seeing Joey catch fish. The fish were always hungry, and I knew we would catch a lot. Watching a trout rise to a dry fly was spectacular. You would see the pop on the surface and the metallic flash as it dove to the bottom and leaped out of the water, trying to spit the hook.

We glided so peacefully along the banks, almost in a dream world. Time passed so smoothly as the miles passed by. There was no watch to look at, only the sound of the paddle pushing the water by the canoe. You didn't realize that only a few yards up the bank were houses, roads, and people going about their daily business. This was only the beginning of our trip, and the feeling that came over you was wonderful. I could only imagine where this canoe and the waters that we would explore would take us.

Back to Camp

I CALLED OUR RIDE, John, and told him we were at White Hole, approaching the next pickup point. About a half hour later, he arrived with his truck, and we loaded up the canoe. It was getting close to lunchtime, and I said, "Let's catch our lunch," thinking that we were right on the river, so why not give it a try?

This time, we grabbed our spinning rods with a small spinner lure. The rainbows like to chase something shiny, and this should do the trick. You could see the fish in the pool grouped in a small pod. All he did was flip a cast up above them, and "Bang," Joey had a nice one. We only needed two, so he was done. *Get out of the way so the old man can eat, too,* I thought. It took me three casts, and I had mine, as well.

"Now it's your turn to clean, and I'll cook them," I advised Joey. Fresh trout cook over an open fire in a cast iron pan; man, it doesn't get any better! Toast, potatoes, and coffee rounded out the meal.

The river was still running hard; it was midday, and all five turbines were spinning, providing power for the grid. Joey and I straightened up camp. We had a lot of gear to keep track of. With its four-man capacity, the tent provided ample space for our cots and sleeping bags. We would be living like this for the next three and a half months.

What freedom we had. We didn't have to be anywhere at any time if we didn't want to. A lot of times, we would sleep in the truck at a rest stop when we got tired or could not reach our next destination at a decent hour to fish.

We would just lie across the front and back seats. It was not very comfortable, but it worked.

It sometimes felt like we were two homeless trout bums. What a life—a dream come true with no cares or concerns, no watches to stare at, and no people to report to. I wish it could have lasted forever. The thought of Joey going off to a raging war was in the back of my mind, and I tried not to think about it and didn't talk to him about it.

After lunch and camp clean up, I suggested we take a drive to see if we could find some backwaters that were still. The river would rise several feet during peak times, and it would back up water into usually non-existent coves. This would push the trout into the stiller protested water. I knew a few of these places, so we headed out. We parked on a dirt road and made our way through the tangled brush and weeds.

I heard a lot of mumbling and cussing coming from behind me. Not to mention getting your nine-foot fly rod hung up in the tree branches. I turned around laughing and told Joey to quit being such a girl. Once we popped out on the riverbank, it was a different story. It felt as though I had traveled back in time and stumbled upon a forgotten and concealed lagoon. The water had pushed back about a hundred yards. It flooded a grassy cut between the bank and the main river channel, forming an island in the middle. There were downed logs submerged along with root balls, making it look fishy.

Well, when we looked down into the water, there must have been one hundred trout schooling around in circles. What a sight! Should we cast into that swarm of fish or just watch the event? Joey couldn't stand it any longer, so he popped his line out across this frenzy of fish.

He hooked one, and the rodeo was on. That fish spooked all the rest of them, and it looked like a shotgun blast exiting the head of the pool. He landed the rainbow and released it. He said, "I should have watched them for a little while longer."

I told him, "Life comes along only once, and you experience something spectacular." We looked at each other with a big grin on our faces.

We spent a few more days on the White River in the canoe. I decided to paddle at the back while Joey fished from the front. That way, I could give him some fatherly advice and fishing lessons and laugh at him when he lost a fish. We packed up and headed out to parts unknown!

White Hole on the River

THE FIRST PART of the float trip on the White River would lead us to one of my favorite spots, White Hole. It was named for the pure white limestone that made up a long stretch of the river's bottom. The water's clarity combined with the limestone was amazing. You could see every trout as it sparkled in the water.

There were some huge brown and rainbow trout in the deep pools just sitting there, looking for a meal to move by. Below some riffles, there was a perfect spot in the pool to anchor the canoe and lure one of those monsters with a fly. We rigged up with a sculpin fly that imitated a small catfish-like minnow that the big trout fed on. We could see a large dark shape cursing in the pool. It was a huge brown trout!

Both Joey and I cast up to the head of the pool so the fly would drift naturally into the deeper water. This spot belonged to this trout. My fly passed him with no result. The next cast was Joey's presentation with only a slight glance given by the fish. Then the trout knew we were there.

As if he knew what to do next, this monster put on an underwater exhibition for us. It circled the pool like the predator that he was. The pectoral fins looked like wings spread under his belly and flared out to steer him as he glided effortlessly through his kingdom. Brown, green, and burnt orange spots glistened as the sun penetrated deep into the pool. We just stood there watching the elegance of the creature.

Then, with one powerful flip of his tail, out of the pool and down the river, he went. Joey said, "Did you see that?" What a show we had just witnessed! That was one of the many experiences we would have on this trip.

Well, back in the canoe and down the river we went. This fish was over 30 inches long and was a master of the river. He didn't get that big by chance. The record brown trout is 40.4 lbs. That's right, so the chance of hooking a world-class trout was there. Time on the water and luck is a fisherman's dream.

Looking back on this moment, it was a priceless experience. Later, in White Hole, Arkansas, Debi and I would scatter some of Joey's ashes into this particular water hole. It only seemed fitting that we saw the biggest trout of his life.

Riding the Surge on the White River

AFTER LEAVING White Hole, we fished downstream for a mile or so. The rainbows were biting, and the river flow was smooth. Remember me telling you that the big hydroelectric dam at Bull Shoals Lake regulated this river's water flow? When fishing there, special fishing regulations are written and posted about the sudden water flow surge.

When the gates are opened, and the turbines start increasing water flow, a very loud horn is sounded. Posted warnings are all over the river about the danger of getting caught up in the swift current. That's why you fish early in the morning and get out of there by late morning.

We were several miles ahead of the surge, but you could feel it coming. Suddenly, paddling got a lot easier. The water temperature dropped, and you could feel the coolness coming off the water. I told Joey to get ready for a ride. The river went from a gentle stream to raging rapids in a matter of minutes. It is like surfing in a canoe. Where there was a gravel bar now, white water covered it over.

The water can quickly rise several feet, so you don't want to be wade fishing on the wrong side of the river. We stowed all our gear and got ready for a ride. I was in the back, and Joey was in front. There were several places to pull into to be picked up, so I told him we would go about two miles before we got out.

Hugging the bank is always a good idea because if you tip over, you have a better chance of getting out. The water temperature is in the 50s all year because of the water coming out from the bottom of the dam. Not good for swimming when you are getting swept down the river. It was fun skimming downstream while doing some fancy paddling. We were doing well until a wing dam jutted out into the river. I shouted over to Joey to paddle left, but he went right instead.

Guess what? The current turned the canoe broadside, and water started coming in. Then we were turned around backward. Man, we are going for a swim. I hit three hard strokes on the left side and got us up on the bank.

Joey jumped out, grabbed the front rope, and pulled us up out of the water. He said, "Let's take a break," and I agreed.

So, we sat on the bank and laughed a lot about our first canoe trip on the White River.

Big Horn and Big Bull Moose

JOEY AND I were in Wyoming now, and it was still wild and open! Highway 90 leads us out of Sheridan, which is the gateway to the Big Horn Mountains. Dreams of the early explorers, mountain men, and Indians who roamed this region added to the excitement. Knowing that Buffalo Bill Cody and Teddy Roosevelt explored and hunted these mountains—well, it was a dream come true!

Speaking of Buffalo Bill, we made a special trip to Cody, Wyoming, just to see the Wild West Museum. That's another story. Now, back to fishing.

We camped up in the mountains and fished the North Tongue River first. The mountains were as rough and rugged as I had imagined. We drove up Hwy. 14 past Elk View towards Burgess Junction before turning onto Alternate Hwy. 14, which led us into the Tongue River drainage.

We set up camp near Little Willow Creek, which meets the Tongue. What a perfect spot, right on the river, with no one around. There were several forestry roads that led to the water, and we had maps to navigate the area. It didn't take us long to hit the water and start casting flies at those cutthroat trout. The water was so clear that you had to approach the pools so as not to spook the trout with your shadow or reflection.

It took some sneaking and casting to get the fish to rise to a fly. You could see the fish, and when they saw you, off they darted. It was a little frustrating for Joey because he was used to catching those stocked hatchery fish from Arkansas. "That's why they call it fishing and not catching," I reminded him.

Personally, I was captivated by the scenery, and the fishing was just a byproduct. "Savor the moment," I told him. "Look around and see the gifts you have been given."

I hooked the first West Slope native cutthroat on a Parachute Madame X fly. Each fly is named either by the bug it resembles or by the man who first tied it. Fly-fishing is a special world that goes back to split bamboo rods and simple reels.

Joey came over to watch as I wet my hands in the cool water, slid the trout gently in, and removed the tiny #20 hook. I held the trophy in the water while he took a few pictures. I thanked the trout for the pleasure and released it back into its world.

I didn't realize it then, but Joey had taken a short video with his cell phone. After his property came back from Afghanistan, Debi and I found it on his phone. What a memory to hear his voice and the excitement he had. You can find the video on the Red Lion Project Facebook page for everyone to watch.

Joey and I fished in that pool, catching trout and enjoying the day together in the mountains. There was plenty of water to cover, with the North and South Tongue coming together for a total of 265 miles before it flowed into the Yellowstone River in southeastern Montana. During our time in the Big Horn Mountains, Joey listened and learned about fly-fishing. There's a simple pleasure in casting the line just right, watching the fly dance on the water's surface.

It's not that hard once you understand that if you can visualize 11:00 and 2:00 o'clock in your mind. Move the rod up to 11:00 and release your cast at the 2:00 position. That's all well and fine if you're not up in a tree branch behind or in front of you.

Needless to say, all of our lessons were accompanied by a lot of laughter on my part as I watched Joey cast his bug. Often, it looked like he was using a bullwhip, not a #6 weight fly rod. Power is not needed in a small brushy stream like the ones we were fishing. I showed him how to read the water by seeing what was on top and understanding the structure on the bottom.

The North Tongue meandered through alder bushes and downed logs. It was an obstacle course. It was a fun experience, complete with some profanity directed at the plants and vegetation! Slowing down and being patient weren't part of this 19-year-old's character. Once he got the idea that nature was in control and we were only guests, things got a little easier.

I did more watching than fishing because watching Joey light up and yell, "Fish on!" was all I was there for. We fished some of the most beautiful areas in the Big Horn Mountains. It was time to move on to our next destination, Cody, Wyoming. On the way out, driving down a forestry road, Joey said, "Stop the Truck—it's a moose!"

The bull was standing just 20 feet off the road! This was one of the most memorable animals we saw. The moose was in the process of shedding the velvet off his antlers. The huge beams on his head were a reddish bloody pink color, with velvet hanging from them. The moose just stood there eating the leaves of an elder bush.

Joey said, "I want to see how close I can get to him to take a picture."

Just as I was about to warn him, he jumped out of the truck and came face to face with that massive creature. Foolish? No fear? Or both? To my surprise, the moose didn't show much interest in him. It would have been a different situation if this occurred a few months later when he was in full rut.

Joey climbed back into the truck and said, "Did you see that?!" His face showed a huge smile, and he was in awe of what he had accomplished.

Black Canyon

IT'S BEEN SAID that half the fun of an adventure is the anticipation of getting there. How would you feel if the first sign you read was "16% Grade Downhill" on a winding mountain road? And, of course, the next sign read, "Use Lowest Gear and Make Frequent Stops If Your Brakes are Failing!"

This was the road we took to our next fishing destination, the Gunnison River in Colorado. The magazine articles had warned us in advance about the roller coaster ride to the bottom. But as we looked over the canyon wall to the tiny sliver of water below...well...was it going to be worth the ride?

I asked Joey if he was ready, and he replied, "HELL YES!" Next, I asked him if he wanted to drive, and he said, "HELL NO, you have it all!"

With the truck in first gear, we began our descent. There wasn't much room for two-way traffic, so oncoming vehicles had you hugging the inside wall of a solid rock wall. To top that off, there were several people on bicycles going up and down the road. Their helmets and knee pads wouldn't do them much good if they went over the edge. We got close to a few of them and got a friendly one-fingered wave. The pucker factor is part of the ride in life for all of us.

We were both relieved when the road leveled out at the bottom. The river was a boulder patch with a lot of pocket water to pick your way along. We rigged up with a hopper and two midge-nymph droppers. There were rainbow and brown trout in this river, so I figured this setup would give the fish something to look at. And man, was I right.

Looking through polarized sunglasses, you could see the browns tailing in the side water near the banks! It was tight fishing along most of the river, with a lot of brush and overhanging trees blocking our casts. It's easier to *show* someone how to cast in a place like this *rather than tell* them.

We were standing side by side when we spotted a brown a few yards upstream. First, I had to cast downstream, flip the line up above and in front, and high-stick the leader so the fly line would not spook the fish. This seems like a lot, but it is really simple. The hopper drifted by, and the brown took the first dropper and went downstream.

I called for my net boy as the trout hugged the bottom and crossed over to the other side of the stream. My fishing guide, Joey, gave me instructions on how to play the fish. He moved downstream and, like a tag team, wrestled and scooped the trout into the net. "Wow," he said, "this is great."

We released the trout, and then I told Joey it was his turn. "No problem," he said. "I can do this!"

"We'll see," I replied. "You're up, buddy; let's see what you got."

I knew this was going to be a rodeo for him, so I was going to have some fun with this. His first cast, on the back cast, clipped the gravel bank behind him. He flipped the cast upstream to a waiting trout, but there was no fly on the leader. It had snapped off when it hit the rocks.

"Great cast," I said. "Try it again, and maybe the fish might see it this time." Joey was so focused on the fish biting that he didn't realize the fly had disappeared. I forgot to mention that he had a strike indicator above a size 14 nymph on his line, so seeing the fly was not that easy.

I started laughing uncontrollably, and he looked at me and said, "What's wrong with you?"

I said, "It might help if you had a hook on the end of your line!" He held up his rod, and if I had had a camera, it would have been a priceless picture. I couldn't resist telling him that all that practice casting looked good, but the fish were still laughing.

With some grumbling and a few choice words mumbled under his breath, he re-tied a bug on his leader. The fly landed where it was supposed to, but the brown ignored it. With all the casting and water wiping, the fish had had enough. I suggested we move upstream and look for some fishtailing in the side pockets.

We slipped along the bank, and across the other side, I spotted a nice brown lying there waiting for lunch. I asked Joey if he wanted to try again, but he told me to go ahead. With a couple of false casts, I had the hopper-dropper right where I wanted. The trout darted out of its hiding place and smacked the nymph dropper. The fish darted downstream, staying close to the bottom and using the current to escape. Joey yelled, "I got the net."

And I cautioned him, "Don't let this one get away; it's huge!"

I believe my son found it more entertaining when I waded out to his chest to catch this huge fish with a net. "I got him," he yelled one more time from behind that colossal smile—one that I miss dearly. He made it back to shore, and we admired the 20-inch brown trout male in all its colors. Joey unhooked the beast and gently slipped it back into the stream.

What a team we made; a father and son making memories that would last a lifetime. We fished most of the day. The steam had endless water to cast a fly and to watch a hungry trout rise to the surface and slurp it down. Joey even managed to catch a few rainbows, which made it a successful day.

By then, it was time to set up camp. The sun was starting to go down over this deep canyon, so we found a spot. Setting up came as second nature now, so we finished quickly and started dinner with burgers and beans on the menu.

We just sat there afterward, watching the sun drop over the rim of the canyon and the stars come out. Steam rushed by, playing music only we could understand. What a journey we were on, and sharing the story with others is one of my greatest dreams.

Charlie and Joey

YOU DON'T REALLY know how much you miss people until they are gone. Missing the conversations you had and the good times you remembered leaves a void that cannot be filled. Perhaps this is why I'm writing about them: to ensure they're never forgotten.

Charlie Tyler and I started our relationship some 30 years ago with his brother, Matt, who introduced us. Right from the start, we hit it off great! We had so much in common, particularly our love of the outdoors, hunting, and fishing. It seemed like that was the sole focus of our conversations.

The friendship grew, and he and his wife, Norma, visited us here in Texas. We returned the favor by going to Wisconsin. The place that bounded this friendship was the ranch property we owned outside the small Texas hill country town of Rock Springs. Charlie and Norma were avid hunters, and I invited them down one fall.

I had standing orders from my wife that if I went to the ranch, I had to take all five kids with me. This is where Joey and Charlie first met. Joey took a shine to Charlie and would tag along when they went to the hunting stand. I think Joey was about nine years old then, and even at that age, he was fascinated with the outdoors. What better mentor could a young boy have to spend time with, listen to, and learn from? This became an annual trip for both of us.

Joey never forgot the week-long trip to Charlie's cabin on a lake in upper Wisconsin. That trip made such a lasting impression. At that time, we fished for bass and northern pike, hoping to catch a Muskie. We caught plenty of fish, but not the big monster we were after.

The next day, Charlie asked if we wanted to go shooting. Without hesitation, Joey was headed for the truck. Charlie had brought along a special rifle: a Winchester Model 1894, chambered in .45 Long Colt. Charlie and Joey walked out to the 100-yard line and placed several clay pigeons on the ground. We all met back at the shooting bench as Charlie described the rifle to Joey.

The rifle was an *original* Winchester saddle ring carbine. It sported a 16-inch barrel and a big loop lever like the ones John Wayne and Chuck Connors used in their Western movies. Joey's interest really perked up then! Charlie shot first, breaking four out of four targets. I went next and did the same. This was with open sights, mind you. Not bad for two old men with poor vision!

As we took turns shooting, Charlie and I kept taking glancing back at Joey. You could see Joey's anticipation mounting as he waited for his turn. He loaded the rifle and cycled the action with the large circle loop lever, a huge smile across his face.

"Just like the cowboys!" he exclaimed. He aimed the rifle, and the hammer fell. Another clay bird turned into dust. He looked at us, almost in disbelief, but quickly said, "How about that, Daddy-O?"

After our shooting session, Charlie handed him the rifle and said, "It's yours now." That kid was speechless! The grin on his face got even bigger. What a gift for a boy to have been given to him by a great man, a lifelong friend.

The rifle now hangs on the wall next to Joey's picture, next to a brass plate with his and Charlie's names engraved on it. I take it down occasionally, cycle the action, look down the sights, and remember both of them shooting and having so much fun that day. Until we meet again, Joey and Charlie.

Get Lost in Montana

JOEY AND I had just returned to Montana from our fishing excursion into Canada. Remember the passports we got before starting on this journey? We went fishing in British Columbia, then headed into Alberta and explored the Old Man River before somehow returning to B.C. and ultimately ending up in Libby, Montana. By this time, I truly believe we were lost!

However, the great thing about this is—we did not care where we were! I think this is when Joey fell in love with Montana. I know I sure did. If you can understand the feelings of dreaming, reading about, and wishing to go to a place, then suddenly you are finally there. The amazing amount of water to fish in this area is astounding. We fished the Kootenai River in B.C. and then again in Montana. This river flows from Canada into the U.S. and then back into Canada. The fish don't care which country they are in!

We pulled into town and stopped at a motel. It was about time because neither of us could stand the smell that had accumulated after several days without a shower. We would look at each other and ask, "Is that you or me?"

I checked in and asked the clerk if there was a church service going on across the street on a Wednesday evening. "No," the clerk said. "That's the DWI and drug abuse mandatory meeting for all the drunks and dopers arrested last winter." The cabin fever, drugs, alcohol, and rock and roll are a big part of the long winters up there.

It reminded me of a time when we were parked at a truck stop one night, sleeping in the truck, and heard a loud crash. Along with all the other truckers, Joey and I woke up to witness what had occurred. No one could find the source of the loud noise, so everyone went back to sleep. The next morning, we awoke to police lights flashing and officers walking in the woods past the intersection.

The previous night, a drunk had missed the turn, went airborne, and hit several trees with his truck, yet walked away from the crash. I guess angels watch over little kids and drunks.

It was time to plan our next adventure, so I looked at our map and saw a river called the Yaak. Who could resist fishing in the river with a name like that? We quickly drove up Highway 2 North and soon arrived in the town of Yaak, which comprised only four buildings.

Yaak, Montana, nestles in the farthest northwestern corner of the state, next to Canada and Idaho. What a setting to spend time on a remote river with no pressure from anything or anybody. This reminds me of a quote from Henry David Thoreau:

> *Many go fishing all their lives without knowing that it is not fish they are after.*

We found such a spot there, and I will revisit that place again to refresh the memories of such a simple time. There were plenty of fish to catch in the Yaak River, including the rare red band rainbow, as well as charr and brook trout weighing up to three pounds!

The river itself is breathtaking! It mainly flows over solid bedrock. The jagged rock juts out in geometrical patterns, cracked and broken by eons of water and weather. The pockets and pools that are formed look like a stone mason quarried and put them in place. The water was crystal clear, then foaming and swirling between the rock formations, making our casts more difficult. We had to be careful crossing between the sharp points to reach the fishy water. But man, was it worth it!

There were trout in about every pool you dropped a fly into. I encourage readers of this adventure to look up these places because words have not been invented to describe them. It's a common occurrence for me to do this, and I have to pinch myself to believe we were actually there!

Those red band rainbows had a rosy brick red strip running along their lateral line. Joey caught the first one, and what a beauty it was. We admired it and released the trophy back to its home. They are protected, and keeping such a colorful fish should be left to bread.

We continued rock hopping most of the day. The pure ruggedness and serene quiet of the area gave you such a feeling of peace. Often, I didn't cast a line; I just listened to the sound of the water as it flowed by. As was said earlier, it was not about fishing. Very seldom does an experience like this happen, where a father and son are together in a place like this.

Sun Valley, Idaho—The Big Wood River

FISHING IN DIFFERENT PLACES is not always what you picture it to be. The Big Wood River runs through one of the country's most popular ski resorts near Ketchum, Idaho. Fishing your way through downtown Bellevue, Hailey, and Ketchum will lead you to Sun Valley. If you get hungry, stop into Grumpy's or Lefty's for a beer and burger, and get right back into the water to catch an 18-inch Rainbow.

This area was very welcoming and a pleasant break from sleeping in the truck and eating canned food. This entire trip was like a dream vacation for a fisherman. I'll repeat it: Thank God for a loving wife and mother who kept money on my debit card.

One could look up from the stream and see multi-million-dollar homes and ski resorts while snagging a trout simultaneously. Joey and I loved the wilderness here and were planning to head up into the Copper Basin and fish for the grand slam of a trout. That "slam" would comprise Brook trout, Mountain Whitefish, Rainbow trout, and the Snake River fine-spotted cutthroat trout. What a menagerie of fish swimming in the same eco-system!

I was excited to start, so we headed out of Ketchum, up Lake Creek Road, and made it to a dirt road. My truck's front end was acting mushy, so we stopped, and guess what? A flat tire. This was a new 2007 GMC truck, and once I looked at the tire, a few choice words were uttered! It was unbelievable that they had only regular two-ply street tires on my 4x4 truck!

We changed the tire, threw the flat in the truck bed, and went fishing. I'll literally be kicking tires when I buy a new truck again. We stopped and bought new off-road tires on the way back into town. This was the second flat on this truck in one week.

We would fish four creeks in the basin: Lake Creek, Taylor Creek, Sawmill Gulch, and one that didn't have a name. These little creeks were full of small trout, so we set up with a green drake cripple and hair-wing duns. Those pesky Brookies would strike at anything. Catching them was so much fun; we even made a game of trying not to catch them by pulling the fly away right when they struck. However, those fish would literally jump out of the water after the fly.

Now that playtime was over, we had to get serious about catching the slam! Rainbows were the next fish we went after, and we hooked plenty of them. Next, we had to change flies and tie a bead head nymph on the dry to catch the Whitefish. Joey gloated after catching the first one. Not to be shown up by this rookie fly fisherman, I yelled out for him, "Get the net! Fish on!" and had him assist me in landing the Snake River fine-spotted cutthroat.

The landscape changed dramatically as we continued fishing higher and higher into the mountains. It started along the tree-lined grassy banks, much like you see on most postcards with the perfect scenic settings. The higher we got, the less vegetation and more rock we saw. In some places, it looked like the moon's surface with barren rock and a sliver of a stream flowing downhill to meet up with a larger creek than the river below. From up here, you could see the workings of nature coming together and joining forces.

What a sight it was from 12,078 feet above sea level near Hyndman Peak! As we fished up one of the streams, the water just disappeared into the ground. There was no more snow on the mountaintops to replenish it. The seasons come and go in the mountains in an endless cycle, and to witness this makes you think about your own life: How many seasons do you have, and what have you done to help others on their journey?

A parting shot from Ketchum was of us visiting the Hemingway Memorial. Ernest Hemingway made his final home in this town. I explained who he was and some of his writings to Joey. Having read most of Hemingway's work, I found it great to have the opportunity to visit the site. It was a simple place with a bronze bust of his head atop a stone pillar. A small stream diverted from the main creek and flowed alongside it. Inscribed on a plaque were the words:

> Best of all, he loved the fall,
> the leaves yellow on the cottonwoods,
> leaves floating on the trout stream,
> and above the hills,
> the high blue windless sky
> ...Now, he will be a part of them forever.

Joey and I left without saying a word. Until now, I truly did not appreciate what that inscription meant.

The Lochsa River

THERE IS A RIVER in Idaho that holds a very special place in my heart. Joey and I fished the Lochsa River for over 100 miles from its source in the Bitter Root Mountains on the Idaho-Montana border. Every time I think of it, so many vivid memories flow through my mind.

The river starts as a small stream called Crooked Fork and then flows into Colt Killed Creek. This is where the Lewis & Clark Expedition killed a young colt horse to eat to survive. Can you imagine that group of men starving with winter coming on? Call them brave or crazy, but they made it out of there to complete their journey.

Looking at the journey Joey and I took, with a highway running along the river and campsites and small towns dotted along the way, made our trip seem so easy. All we had to worry about was who was going to catch the next fish!

Years later, I revisited this river, but it was to spread some of his ashes in a place he loved so much. I wrote about this journey in a chapter called *The Trail of Ashes*. That was a long time ago, and now the fishing memories keep me coming back to catch one more fish.

The amazing thing about this river is that during the right seasons, you can catch four types of trout: brook, rainbow, cutthroat, and bull. During May, June, and July, salmon were in the river. From September through April, steelhead trout were spawning. You could literally spend an entire year just fishing in this river! We wished we could have experienced all the seasons on the river, which would be a real fish story. Now I have this chance because the Red Lion Project is located so close to this river, just over the next mountain range.

Joey and I started by visiting the fish hatchery located just a short distance from Powell Ranger Station. We looked into the tanks, and there were huge salmon that would be stripped of the milt from the males and eggs from the females. This would be the start of the next generation of fish. They would make their way to the sea some 700 miles away, returning five years later to complete the cycle of life.

Joey popped off, saying, "Man, I wish we could fish here!" I told him we would try our luck in the river in just a little while. He could hardly wait to get in the water.

The ranger giving us the tour said that the fish in the tanks would lose over 30% of their body weight by the time they spawned. The drive and instinct that brings them back to where they were born is astounding. We thanked him for his time, and Joey said that he would love a job like that. I told him, "Maybe someday you will." His love and passion for nature and the outdoors showed me where his heart was. I could only smile and hope he would live the same dream I always wanted.

Well, finally, we got our lines wet! We had both fly and spinning tackle, so today, we decided to use the spinners. It was a great choice, catching dozens of cutthroats. It was fun, but I was hoping Joey would hook a salmon. We changed over to a spinner with a pink and orange body. You could see the fish swimming up through the shallow riffles and then darting into the deep pools. By this time of their journey, the fish would only strike out of reflex rather than feeding.

They say for every 100 casts, you might catch one salmon. There are not very good odds, and there are a lot of sore arm muscles. Wouldn't you know it? I heard that familiar yell, "Fish on!" But this one was even louder than I had ever heard him yell before. The excitement in his voice almost had me walking on water to get over to him with the net! Sure enough, he had one on the line.

We weren't fishing with heavy line, only 10 lb. test, so the battle was on. His drag was screaming with a line headed downstream, and his rod bent in two. I don't know who was more excited, him or me! This was truly a tug of war, with the fish winning.

Joey yelled, "I can't hold him."

I told him to jump in after the fish. Before he could turn the fish, he had to scramble over the rock and down to the gravel bar.

"I got his head turned; get the net ready," Joey proclaimed.

The battle wasn't quite over yet. The salmon saw the net in the water, felt the gravel on the bottom, and took off with another run. The beast was giving up now and slowly glided into the waiting net.

It was a trophy we would never forget. A solid 32 inches of Pacific salmon cradled in a young man's arms. What a moment—frozen in time—but now, to me, as fresh as if it happened yesterday. It was a story to tell all your fishing buddies. The salmon was released back to the river where it belonged, with a few photos and a splash of a tail. Can you believe that was the only salmon we managed to catch on the Lochsa? Some things are meant to be, and this was one of them.

After that fish, what else could anyone want? I know he is fishing in heaven, waiting for me to join him. He has his fly rod with him, which we placed in his coffin. He was cremated, but I kept the fly reel and still use it all the time. We fished and camped along the river, enjoying every moment.

There was very little vehicle traffic on Hwy 12, which runs through some of Idaho's most rugged, beautiful country. About halfway down our route, there were campsites, RV pull-in spots, cabins, and a sort of resort. We decided to get a campsite and stay there for several days. There was also a pretty good restaurant and tackle shop, an all-in-one place in the middle of nowhere. Joey was all for the restaurant after several days of Dad's gourmet cooking.

We went into the bait shop and talked to the manager, who told us of several other places to fish. One sounded interesting: a mountain lake with big brook trout in it. We got the directions, and off we went. We went up a winding mountain road that seemed to wander for miles, and then we came to a huge boulder that partially blocked the road.

As we drove around it, Joey said, "Did you see the other half of that rock sitting above the one that fell?"

I did and said, "What are the chances of that half falling while we are fishing the lake?"

Joey replied, "I don't want to find out; it's a long walk out to get help, and who out here is going to move those rocks to get the truck back?" He had a point, so we turned around and headed back to safer ground!

On the way down, we spotted a small creek and fished it. It was loaded with brook trout. Light fly rods and tiny flies made this a blast. After that, it was back to our base camp for a huge burger, fries, and a couple of beers.

We were a couple of trout bums enjoying every moment and were discussing doing this for a living. Man, what a life that would be: taking other fishermen out exploring and doing something you loved. I could do this now, but I would miss my fishing buddy too much; maybe I will.

As we traveled down the river, it got wider and deeper as it coursed down the valley. This is what postcards are made of; if I were an artist, here's where I would have painted a masterpiece. Pulling off the road into one of the many spots to park was our next fishing hole. There was a giant boulder in the middle of the river, as big as a small house. We just stared at its size and could almost visualize it tumbling down the mountainside with the sound of thunder crashing into the river. It must have made a hell of a splash!

The water was about halfway up this giant piece of granite, and it looked like it was 20 feet deep around it. The rock had been there since the beginning of time. We saw moss, bushes, and a big log that had washed up on it during the spring run-off. I told Joey to change lures, so we both switched to a Rapala. Maybe we could entice a big bull trout to take the bait. My first cast and an 18-inch cutthroat smacked the lure. It put up a good fight and was released.

Remember how I told you about Joey's lack of fishing fineness? He said, "Move over, old man, and let me try this spot."

I obliged, and he let fly with his first and only cast in this pool. Would you believe he snagged the boulder? "Great cast," I laughed. "Now, how are you going to get it back?"

"No problem. I'll yank on it, and it will come loose." He yanked, and the line broke!

"Now, you owe me a lure!" I still laugh about that cast, and many like it. I went back to the rock a few years later, and you could see it still stuck there as a reminder that we were here.

We fished the river for several miles a day and made it all the way down to Orofino, Idaho. This is the salmon capital of the Pacific Northwest. Everything here revolves around salmon, and it's where the Dworshak National Hatchery is located. Remember the salmon in the catch pens at the headwaters? Well, here's where those tiny fish are raised. Joey and I took a break from fishing, if you could believe that, and toured the hatchery.

The complex was set up in different stages according to the size of the salmon being raised. Along with salmon, steelhead trout are also raised here. The conservation effort is amazing. There are millions of fish in the huge indoor and outdoor concrete tanks. We watched the feeding, and the fish swarmed wildly when the pellets were mechanically dispersed. Joey's eyes lit up, and he said, "This is what I want to do for a living."

All these fish are released into the Clearwater River and return to the source of the Lochsa. What an experience and education we were getting. We decided to get a motel room, clean up, and plan the next part of our expedition. Happy fishing!

Old Faithful in Yellowstone

I'M GRATEFUL for John Colter, an early explorer who likely discovered Yellowstone in 1807. Yellowstone was set aside as a national treasure by President Ulysses S. Grant as the first National Park in the world. Colter was part of the original Lewis and Clark expedition. He went back to civilization and told about it; people said he was mad and called it "Colter's Hell!" They could not believe it existed.

I recommend everyone visit to see the marvels of nature. Sure, we would fish, but being there made you feel so small and humble. I can only picture how this place looked before it was discovered. The park covers parts of three states: Wyoming, Montana, and Idaho. Nowhere else in the world can you find a natural setting as vast and spectacular as this 3,000-square-mile area.

Joey and I arrived midday, and even before we found a campsite, we had to see the Old Faithful Geyser. It's easy to find; all signs point to it. I parked the truck, went to sit down in the observation area, and right then, the geyser went off. What perfect timing!

It was a great way to explore the park. The geyser goes off between 30 minutes and an hour and a half. Sitting there, feeling the ground shake, watching and hearing it explode, transports you to a prehistoric era. The hissing coming from deep underground left no doubt that you were sitting on top of a volcano. Then, seeing the water and steam blasting 90 to 180 feet in the air almost made you want to run for cover!

Most of the time we spent there was exploring the park's wonders. Allow me to take you on a visual trip as best I can. If I could put pictures of our adventures in this book, there would not be room for words. After seeing all the natural wonders the park offered, we almost forgot about fishing.

Setting up camp had become easy now, and off we went with a map and eyes wide open. The next stop was the upper and lower falls of Yellowstone. Many artists and photographers have captured the falls. This place is captivating, as your eyes and mind work together like you are in a fantasy dream world. The river and falls start at Yellowstone Lake, just a short distance away. Standing on the lava rock outcropping above the upper falls is beyond breathtaking.

The sound of the cascading water rumbling as it rushes past with immense power is intimidating. The water spills in cascades over the sheer cliffs, their color a vibrant emerald green. Then, it changes to a frosty white on its journey downward to the pool below. Once the flow explodes at the bottom, a cloudy mist forms and drifts downstream. Mixed in all of this is a prismatic rainbow flashing in the sunlight.

After seeing this, we had to go to the lower falls. Once there, a trail leads to a meandering staircase that wines and twists down several hundred feet to the base of the falls and canyon below. Those in Hawaii who have ever hiked the Stair Way to Heaven would love this hike down—but of course, you had to hike up!

Taking your time is a must because of all the different views you have of the falls as you descend. When you feel the temperature drop as you get closer to the bottom, it indicates that the water is melted ice and snow from the mountain tops. Once we reached the bottom of the falls, a cold mist surrounded us.

Words can't capture the emotions experienced in a place like this. Joey and I just looked at each other in total awe. The image of this place will always be locked in my mind, along with the son I shared it with. We walked down to the river and dipped our hands in it. A chill came over us, I think, more from the place we were in rather than the cold water dripping from our hands. It is times like this that you wish would last forever.

The climb back up took about a half hour, with Joey leading the way. You lose track of time when exploring this wonderful place, but it was now time for some lunch. After that, we went off to see another amazing sight. Our plans were to cover as much of the park as we could in a week. That was not enough time!

Next was the Grand Prismatic Spring. This pool was gin clear, reflecting the blue sky from above. The minerals that lined the bottom were colors we had never seen. The blue, green, and gold, with the sun's reflection, dazzled your eyes.

It was tempting to reach down and touch the water to see if it was real. However, you could not; there was a railing on the walkway several feet from the pool and signs in big, bold letters stating caustic water and a temperature of 199 degrees! *Wow, there are many dangerous places in the park,* I thought! The water spilled over the edges of the pool and flowed into the Yellowstone River. This has been going on for a long time before man existed. The park is a thermal extravaganza, and there was much more for us to explore.

Next were the Bubbling Mud Pots. The site is a steamy, mucky, oozing, smelly spot. A sulfur odor fouled your nose, depending on which way the wind was blowing. The gases that percolated from deep underground, forced up through the mud, made music. The tempo and beat as the bubbles of gas popped to the surface were so random.

If you listened closely, the sounds coming from the mud pots played a symphony for you. Joey said, "You can almost hear the earth telling you a story," and I had to agree. He was one of the few people in my life who understood many of the simple things that surround us.

The Petrified Forest was an amazing stand of stone columns. The ancient trees date back to 50 million years ago, proof positive that the world was a much different place. Walking up and touching the wood that was transformed into solid stone made me envision dinosaurs roaming this land.

We would later visit an area called Thermopolis, Wyoming, where an active dig site is unearthing dinosaurs. The Big Horn River flows through there, and hot springs are available at Hot Springs State Park. As mentioned earlier, this journey we took together was a great learning experience and bonding that will forever be in my heart and soul until we meet again. We're not finished with Yellowstone yet!

Everywhere we went in Yellowstone, we saw amazing natural phenomena. Joey and I were simply looking for a place to fish. But every time, we would get sidetracked by another attraction, drawing us to it. We drove by the sign for Mammoth Hot Springs and Limestone Terraces, and off we went down another trail leading to something magnificent.

The hot springs were bubbling out of the earth, carrying liquefied limestone. It had been flowing forever, forming layer upon layer of mineralization. The terraces cover a large area and flow downhill, so the water carrying the mineral-rich mixture coats the formations continually. The formations are a whitish-yellow color and are rounded smoothly from the constant movement of the water. The earth is in a continual flux, building and destroying itself. We were there only a short time, marveling at what it had done.

Finally, it was time to go fishing! Driving along a park road, I spotted a meandering stream flowing through a grassy meadow. We got ready with our fly rods in hand and approached the stream. There was an abundance of wildlife spread all over the park. It seemed like the animals were tame, but they were far from that!

In the distance, there were elk, with bulls in velvet. To be even this close was a thrill in itself. There was a herd of bison grazing along the other side of the stream. The cow bison had newborn calves alongside them. The calves were playful and romped around. I told Joey if they stayed on the other side, we would be alright.

Well, the longer we fished, the closer they got. Then, a few of the cows crossed the stream, followed by the calves. I said, "It's time to get out of here!" I didn't want to get between a mama and her baby; being stomped was not on our fishing list!

In addition to the animals, there were other hazards in the park. The toxic compounds coming up from underground and the high water temperatures were posted on signs all over; we fished in one such place. There was a hot spring bubbling out of the ground and flowing into the Yellowstone River. When the hot water mixed with the glacial water, a huge steamy fog covered the river. It is amazing to me that with this mix flowing into the river, you could catch trout a short distance downriver. Adaptation is nature's way, and this was proof.

In almost all areas of the park, the required fishing is "catch and release," but in Yellowstone Lake, you can keep lake trout. So that was our next spot to fish. The lake is part of an enormous volcanic crater. We found boats available for rent, so we took one out to see what we could catch. The tackle shop guide said that vertical gigging with a spoon worked well. I used a red-eyed wiggler, and Joey had a red-and-white daredevil.

I was at the front of the boat, with Joey positioned at the back. Suddenly, I heard the familiar yell, "Fish on!" My son had snagged a good one. In a short time, the five-pound trout was in the boat, and we had our dinner for the evening. Simple memories like this one last a lifetime, and I'm thankful for every moment. "Take a kid fishing" is what I tell all dads to do with their children.

We fished throughout the park and enjoyed catching the native cutthroat trout, except they were tiny. Some of the fish weren't even six inches long. I remember Joey setting the hook on one of these dinks. The fish sprang out of the water, glided through the air, disconnected in mid-flight, and dropped into the thick brush. Fly-fishing is a finesse sport that involves delicate casting and controlling the power of the rod. I guess Joey didn't learn that part. I asked him if he was really *fly-fishing* or perhaps *flying fish*!

After that episode, I had to sit down on the bank until I quit laughing. My son was a little frustrated and started walking along the river, kicking dried buffalo chips (dried poop) into the river and watching it float downstream. I watched this for a while and told him to knock it off.

Well, he didn't, and the next thing I heard was, "OH crap!" which was followed by more expletives. Yes, he kicked a patty that seemed dry on the surface but was actually green inside. Joey was wearing his sneakers and had splattered buffalo dung all over his shoes and legs.

The look on his face was priceless, and I laughed until I cried. All I could say was, "I told you so!"

The next thing I knew, Joey was in the cold water, trying to wash off his prize. I yelled over to him, "Your new name is Chief Buffalo Chip!" He had to laugh as he cleaned up his mess.

Yellowstone has some special surprises if you don't watch where you step. That week went by quickly, and soon, we were off to our next stop: Cody, Wyoming.

Our Oasis in the Desert

TO ME, the North Platte River near Casper, Wyoming, is a desert oasis. Such names as the Miracle Mile, Grey Reef, and Fremont Cannon are the mecca for hard-core trout fishermen worldwide. This river starts in the high mountains in Colorado at 12,000 feet, flows into the Missouri, next into the Mississippi, and finally ends up in the Gulf of Mexico. What a journey as it starts as a tiny snowflake, melting in the spring, forming a stream, and then flowing along its course all the way back to the ocean.

The history of the river involving white explorers began in 1811 with Wilson Price Hunt of the Astor Expedition and the expanding fur trade. What a time that had to be; you could almost visualize mountain men cutting new trials through the region as you fished from its banks. By 1824, these trappers and traders were having Rocky Mountain rendezvous along its waters.

If you looked hard enough, you could still see them dressed in buckskin with fur hats and a flintlock rifle slung across their shoulders. Many times, as Joey and I talked, we both wished that we were alive back then. Our fishing expedition was a history lesson almost everywhere we went.

Fishing along the North Platte was more civilized than most of the places we had been. Towns like Casper, Alcova, Medicine Bow, and Powder River were nearby, and the river flows right through downtown Casper. The names of the towns bring up visions of famous men like Buffalo Bill Cody and later western cowboys riding the range herding cattle.

We stopped at a fly shop to get information on public access to the river. These fellows were real trout bums! Looking at all the pictures of giant trout that were caught in the river made you ask, "Where did you catch them?"

The owner and two guides were purists when it came to the Platte. All the fish on the wall were released back into the river so others could catch them. There were some hogs posted there! They were very helpful in giving us local maps of the river and what flies were working. Naturally, we had to stock up on the bugs while we were there.

One guide showed us pictures of huge browns and rainbows that he caught in Argentina. He explained that he guides in Argentina during the winter months because it's summer down there. Joey and I both said, at almost the same time, "What a life that would be!" Well, after that visit, we were ready to hit the water.

Wyoming Fish & Game really takes care of the outdoorsmen. The maps were great, and the public fishing areas were well-marked. We fished in all the well-known areas, but the best and most memorable spot was right in the city limits of Casper. We pulled into a small parking area next to a vehicle bridge that crossed the river. There was a nice pool under the bridge with riffles above and below, leading into another deep pool. It looked like a good spot to start. We geared up and were soon wading up to about knee level. With a flick of the wrist, Joey's fly landed in the riffles above the pool and drifted perfectly into the foam line at the edge of the bank.

With a gulp and splash, a big rainbow took the fly and headed deep into the pool. He was looking back at me with the usual huge smile! I said to him, "This time, I saw the entire take." It was a good run, and the trout jumped and did its usual acrobatic tricks before he reeled it in, and I netted it. The fish measured an honest 18 inches! Not bad for the first cast.

By this time in our journey, Joey had almost forgotten about his injured hand and was turning into a pretty good fly fisherman. He should be, with thousands of casts and an untold number of flies stuck in trees and bushes and clipped off on rocks! As we fished under the bridge, passing cars honked, and you could see a hand waving. A school bus full of kids went overhead, and the same thing happened with hands waving and kids yelling, "Did you catch one yet?"

It was clear that there were many fishermen in the area. It was a good feeling to see and hear this.

The Old Man River

WE HAD finally arrived! It was a river that I had only read about, and now Joey and I were standing on the bank stringing our fly rods. What a place nestled in the Canadian Rockies in the untamed wilderness next to the border of British Columbia. The crystal-clear water with a washed gravel bottom and rugged bedrock was a fisherman's dream. You could see the trout in the shallower side water; then it plunged into deep green pools where the bull trout lurked.

The river was named for Na'pi, the Great Spirit and protector in the Piegan native Indian legend. It was like stepping back in time and discovering a new place. How many opportunities in a lifetime would you have the chance to do something like this? I told Joey this as we looked at what we were doing, and I knew *he knew* what I was talking about.

There are three kinds of people in the world: those who make it happen, those who watch it happen, and those who are asking what happened. There's nothing like that first cast drifting a big hooper and seeing a trout strike. Well, Joey did just that, catching a nice 18-inch cutthroat trout. The smile on his face was priceless! We were both having the time of our lives. He landed the fish and quickly released it.

I moved upstream and cast into the edge of a large pool. I got a strike, a small rainbow. As I was playing it in, I saw a dark shadow dart out of the deep pool and grab the trout sideways in its mouth. I was startled at first, and then the tug of war began. It was a huge bull trout trying to eat my trout!

It acted like a pit bulldog that would not let go once it clamped its jaws. I yelled for Joey to come quick and see this. Here he came running down the riverbank, yelling, "What's the matter?"

I said, "It's a bull trout, and it has my fish in its mouth."

He got there just in time to see the big bull coming to the surface as I reeled both fish in.

All of a sudden, the bull let go and gave me a chewed little rainbow. Since I couldn't release it, we kept it for our shore lunch. Having this happen was quite a thrilling experience! That made the trip to the Old Man River worth every mile getting there. We spent time camping and fishing along a 30-mile stretch of the river, where Joey successfully caught multiple bull trout using a long black streamer that drifted deep into the dark waters.

I enjoyed watching him battle these big aggressive fish and seeing the accomplishment when he landed them and set them free. By now, that injured hand was becoming a faint scar, and the fishing that I hoped would make it work again was better than any therapy he could do.

Camping On the Journey

Joey and I camped almost everywhere we went fishing. We wouldn't have had it any other way. Three and a half months in tents, under the stars, and in the back seat of the pickup truck was a real experience. Being this close to nature, in some of the most beautiful and stunning places in America, made us feel part of the earth we slept on.

Gazing up into the heavens and seeing stars you could almost touch was so peaceful. The Milky Way was like a faint cloud drifting through the night sky. Shooting stars falling from the sky that looked like they fell to earth just over the next mountain ridge keep you scanning the darkness for one more. On special nights when the moon was full, you could read a book. On the opposite side of that, when there was a new moon, you could hardly see your hand in front of your face. The night sounds moved all around us, waking with a start, hoping it was not a bear or wolf looking for a meal. The truck was a great place on nights like that.

We often spent the night at truck stops, waiting until the 18-wheelers began their engines in the morning. The roar of a diesel engine cranking up would rattle the truck windows. I don't think there were any other fathers and sons experiencing something like this. You talk about a time of bonding that I hoped would never end, and so did Joey. We talked about the future and places we would like to go, like Alaska and the province of Labrador in Canada. We were fishaholics addicted to the yank of a line and the bend of a fishing pole.

I remember years later talking to one of his Marine buddies, who said all Joey talked about were the places I took him and the great times we had. He said that Joey didn't know why I did it for him, but he was eternally grateful that I did. That made all this worthwhile. The Marine also told me that Joey wanted to take me somewhere special or buy me a pistol to show me how much he loved hanging around with his old man.

I must have known deep down that something was going to happen, and this time together was all that we would have. I have some words of advice for the dads and moms out there: Love your kids, spend time with them, and teach them what you have learned the hard way. Don't be too busy with life getting in the way.

But I digress. Back to camping!

We were up in the mountains in Idaho, in an area that looked like a desert. It was dry, very dry, in early August, and we were alone in a small mountain creek. We fished the stream and caught enough brook trout for dinner. After that, we set up our one-man lightweight tents to spend the night.

The tents went up fairly easily, with thin fiberglass tubing supporting the canvas. There was just enough room to slide your sleeping bag in and lie down. During the night, I felt cold, but I just turned over and dozed off until daylight. I awoke to the sound of hilarious laughter outside my tent. During the night, the supports collapsed, and so did the tent, which is why I felt cold at night.

I crawled out of the tent with a damp, wet sleeping bag wrapped around me, along with the tent on top. Joey was still laughing, saying, "Whatcha do, wet the bed? Hur, hur, hur!"

I learned the hard way that even in a dry climate, dew forms, and your breath creates moisture inside a tent. It was a lesson well learned, and I was lucky the temperature was in the 60s. He had a good laugh, and I told him we were swapping tents that night.

Shattered Hopes and Dreams

If I ever go to war, Mom, please don't be afraid. There are some things I must do to keep the promise that I made. I'm sure there will be some heartache, and I know that you'll cry tears. But your son is a Marine now, Mom, and there is nothing you should fear. Signed, LOVE, JOEY.

Hog Wild

I USED TO RECEIVE a lot of unexpected phone calls from Joey whenever he had some crazy story to tell me about something outrageous he had done. This call was no exception. It started out as usual, with him saying, "Hey, Dad, guess what I just did?"

To which I would reply, "OK, I already don't believe it! But go ahead and tell me."

He got a kick out of always playing the guessing game to amaze me about his latest accomplishment. I knew how much he loved the outdoors, and every adventure seemed more intense than the last. But on this particular call, his next sentence really got me going.

"I just hunted a wild hog and got one with a spear," he bragged.

"Yeah, right, like I'm going to believe that one," I replied.

"For real!" Joey said.

"Alright, tell me the entire story; this should be a good one."

Joey began by saying that his group of Marines had been invited to a plantation up on the North Shore. He said the organizer took them out into the jungle and posted them on a perch fixed to a tree above a game trail. They were each given a spear, each one a 10-foot-long shaft tipped with an 18-inch blade.

The Marines were told to stay in the tree until a hog came by, while a plantation worker would walk through the jungle to move the pigs past the hunters. Sure enough, the next thing he saw was a big hog passing under the tree. The spear found its mark, and the hog expired under the tree.

My son told me how much of a rush it gave to hunt with a spear. He was so excited to tell me about that hunting experience. I wish I could have been there.

The guides came by, took the hog, and prepared it for a full-blown Hawaiian Luau. The hog was baked to perfection, wrapped in banana leaves with all the exotic foods to go along with it.

This is what life is all about, I thought, as Joey recalled the details of that experience. I was glad that he was having exciting and intense experiences and sharing them with friends and family. Someday, I might do the same thing here in Texas. I even made one of the same spears and engraved on it: "RED LIONS, USMC" with the Eagle, Globe, and Anchor next to it.

Semper Fi to all our wild Marines.

Our Last Phone Call

Our Oasis in the Desert Masa Qal'ah, Afghanistan, Camp Leatherneck
Unit HMH-363, MAG-24 2D MAW (FWD) II MFF
1-18-2012 0430am, USA TIME

THE PHONE RANG at 0430 a.m. "Hey, Dad, what's up? This is Joey." Long-distance calls from Afghanistan often have a delay in the conversation, but today, it was clear and audible. Joey called home often, and we loved it when he did.

"I have about a month left, and time is going by so fast. I'll be home soon! I talked to my Sgt. Major, and when we get back to Hawaii, I'll be taking 21 days of leave just to unwind. I'm just coming in from a mission last night, and I'm calling you and Mom before I get some sleep. Well, I'll be flying out again tonight..."

Oh, my God. As I write this, I remember a dream I had about this same conversation. The image was so vivid. I was sitting at the kitchen table, writing about Joey's death. If I only could have warned him ...

Debi and I had just watched a movie that evening, but it was different from our usual viewing. The title was *WWJD, What Would Jesus Do?* It was a Christian movie, and no one in the family knew where it came from or how it got into our movie rack.

The theme of the movie was about a minister who lost his family in a tragic car accident, and afterward, he lost his faith in God and became very depressed. The main character was a man portrayed as a drifter and a military veteran, played by actor John Schneider (Bo from the *Dukes of Hazzard*). This movie must have been sent to us, preparing us for the knock on the door that came just minutes later.

Now, looking back, it has been the driving force helping me cope with Joey's loss and the inspiration for founding the Red Lions Project. I'm writing this almost six years after the crash. You have a lot of time to reflect and see things differently with the passing of time.

The knock on the door came at 10:30 on the night of January 18th, 2012. I had already gone to bed, and Debi was in the kitchen washing dishes. She came running into the bedroom saying, "Tom, Tom, wake up! There are *two Marines* at the front door!"

I thought I was dreaming. "Get up, get the keys, and open the door!" Debi screamed.

As I looked through the window, an awful feeling of horror came over me. Two young Marines in their dress blue uniforms stepped in and stood with somber looks on their faces. They looked like statues with a hardened appearance. All I could say was, "No, no, no! Not Joey. Please go away!" The Staff Sgt. was the first to speak.

"Mr. and Mrs. Logan, we are sorry to inform you that your son, Joseph, is dead. His helicopter went down, and there were no survivors."

All I could remember were their faces and holding Debi. We cried and cried, and it would not stop. *I just talked to him a few hours ago,* I thought. *How can this be?* That phone call was different.

During our call, Joey spoke of having a family reunion. To me, that was almost impossible because we had family members all over the country, if not the world. He said that he would take his 21 days of leave and come home, use my truck, and visit family in Oklahoma, New York, Illinois, Virginia, and here in Texas. It was ironic that he had just 30 days left in his tour. I asked him if he would have time to go fishing, and he said, "at least a week." The conversation was all over the map, with some of it not making any sense.

We did not know all the details of what he was doing in Afghanistan, but I had a pretty good idea. The Sergeant would only say "flying" and leave it at that. I had a feeling that things were heating up over there. Joey had previously stated on Facebook that he had a close call three weeks prior to the fatal crash.

After that post, one of his Navy friends posted to him, "What the hell happened?"

Come to find out, he and the same crew put one down hard and all walked away unharmed. After that crash, the crew was grounded, pending an investigation of either *pilot error* or *equipment failure*. It was determined that the landing gear had folded and broken upon landing. But soon, they were cleared to fly again.

I recollect our conversation regarding the incident where I told him he had already fought enough over there. And I told him he should stay on the ground for the remaining month before coming home. He replied to me stoically, saying, "Dad, I can't do that. The men on the ground need us up there watching over them." The honor, courage, and commitment Joey had were only now beginning to sink in.

Marines in his unit told me later that you could not keep the kid out of the air. Joey showed that during his seven-month deployment. He flew 42 combat missions, resupply flights, medevac transport, and carried special-ops units where he was given a Seal Team One coin. Six great Marines died that night. I believe that every time Joe and the crew were up there, they were touched by the hand of God.

But on that fateful night, the Lord took them to guard the gates of Heaven. They all had their guardian angels with them, and I know Joey gave the enemy hell all the way down before they were flown up to Heaven.

I diverged from the night we were notified for a moment, but let's continue. The Marines who showed up on our doorstep had been assigned to us. They were called "CACO" officers, which stood for **C**asualty **A**ssistance **C**alls **O**fficer. They would be with us for several months through the long process that was to follow.

We were given official papers that night that verified his passing. It stated that he died from several blunt trauma injuries. That reality had not and would not sink in. The two Marines were helpless in consoling us, but they tried their best. They had both been to war, and it was just as hard on them as it was on us. They are all brothers, a bond that few men can ever understand.

After they left, we felt *terribly* alone. None of our other five children lived at home; they were all grown. It was too late to call them and tell them the bad news. Debi and I paced around the house, just crying. We went outside and walked around our neighborhood until daylight.

Sometime during the night, I placed two flags in front of our house. I did not even remember doing it. The American flag was placed on the right side of the driveway, and a United States Marine Corps flag that Joey had given me was placed on the left. I grabbed the Marine flag in my fists and yelled at the top of my voice, "God, give him back to us!"

That morning was so very still, with not even the slightest breeze around. The only way I could describe it was serenely quiet and tranquil, and peace seemed to fall over the area. Debi and I were standing in the driveway when, at the same time, we looked across the small creek that crosses the property.

All of a sudden, the tallest live oak tree started swaying back and forth. It was like someone, *Joey, perhaps*, was waving goodbye.

We looked at each other in disbelief. The two flags stood still against the flagpoles. Then, immediately, the Marine flag unfurled and flew at full mast like it was being held between two outstretched arms. From across the distance of the driveway, the American flag lay limp and unmoving.

What had just happened? You judge for yourself. As for me, I know deep in my heart who was there saying goodbye.

Plane Ride to Dover AFB

BY LATE MORNING, the reality of what happened still had not set in. We got a call from our CACO officer, telling us to go to Dover Air Force Base in Delaware to pick up Joey. However, we had no idea what to do. The only time I had seen anything like this was on TV when a soldier's remains were returned to American soil. The flight there was one of the saddest and yet one of the greatest experiences we will ever have.

Debi and I boarded a commercial flight at the Bush Intercontinental Airport in Houston, accompanied by both of our CACO officers. The passengers on the plane knew what had happened. Seeing two grieving parents, accompanied by two Marines, made an impact on their lives as well.

The outpouring of emotion shook me to the very core of my existence. There were many tears shared on that flight. I remember one man wearing his Marine Corps hat as he got up and gave Debi and me a big hug. This was the beginning of our understanding of the brotherhood of the Corps. He simply uttered the words "Semper Fi."

The phrase, "I'm sorry for your loss," must have been repeated by every single soul on that plane. Another man sitting across from me shook my hand and would not let go. He said, "I was in the Army." He knew what loss was.

When we arrived in Philadelphia, we were allowed to leave the plane before anyone else. As we walked off, we were faced with the first winter storm of the season. The snow, ice, and cold immediately took our breath away.

Our CACO SSgt. had a car waiting for us and drove us to Dover AFB. Andi, our youngest daughter, who was also a Marine, was already at the hotel waiting for us. The Marines once again answered the call for her with two Sergeants and her roommate escorting her from Virginia, where she was stationed.

We did not know what to expect. There were so many people helping and taking care of the families of the Fallen. Six men went down, and it seemed the entire country rose up to help us. If you believe in God and Country, this experience will put a burning passion in your heart forever!

I want to give a special thanks to an awesome group of people who were there from the beginning to the end. They're known as "The Friends of the Fallen" and are among the most patriotic people I've ever encountered. The volunteers worked tirelessly at the reception center, meeting the needs of families and loved ones. A special lady was there; her name was Karen Mordus, and she was the leader of the group.

Karen has such compassion and the biggest heart we have ever seen. She was so kind and understanding to Debi and me. She has since become a lifelong friend.

During our four days in Dover, Karen and I talked at length many times. One day, she said that Joey had to be a very special person, judging by his parents. And she was correct—he was surely one of a kind, with such a big heart and courage of a lion.

One morning, Karen handed me a gold coin in the shape of a large dog tag. I was taken aback by her gesture and studied the coin in disbelief! It was a coin honoring Four-Star General James Amos, the 35th Commander of the Marine Corps. General Amos had made "winning Afghanistan" his top priority upon being commissioned as the 35th Commander of the Corps. He was highly decorated and proudly led the Marines until relinquishing his command in the fall of 2014.

The coin had been given to Karen for her loving care and dedication to the Fallen. She had helped so many in their time of need. She told me, "This is for your son's service and paying the ultimate price for his country."
Clutching that coin in my hand, I vowed to never let it go. Thinking about her giving me this, I can't help but wonder what she was feeling. She had

earned it more than I will ever know. I will honor and cherish this coin and what it represents.

    Semper Fi. Any Marine who sees this coin will understand!

Too Little, Too Late

FOLLOWING SEVERAL MONTHS of waiting, the White House's response to our son's death lacked compassion and respect. The President's letter, delivered in such a way, made it clear they didn't view Joey's death as the significant sacrifice it was to this country. The Commander and Chief had failed to recognize him and the thousands of soldiers fighting for our country.

Only a handful in Washington genuinely understand the meaning of a genuine American Hero. It's not the movie stars you watch or politicians discussing the War on Terror. Our young men and women are losing their lives for leaders who prioritize fame and celebrity status over everything.

Most of our leaders have never even served in the U.S. military and have no idea of the respect that our troops have for this great country. What our soldiers do every day in these ugly foreign wars where the enemy has no rules is unbelievable. Have our leaders ever had to fight for their lives or the lives of their fellow soldiers? Of course, the answer is a resounding "No."

After receiving the form letter from the White House, delivered out of the back of a UPS truck, like junk mail, I had to write a response. Even James, our neighbor and the UPS driver who delivered the letter, knew what it was about based on the return address. Our area congressman, Kevin Brady, delivered my letter to Washington, D.C., and surprisingly, I received a response. However, the disrespect in their reply was appalling!

How can they wear smiles on TV while our soldiers are brought home in boxes, shattered? The initial contact we got from Washington following my reply to their letter was a phone call. But it wasn't the President who reached out—it was a Navy commander who, I believe, had hidden intentions or was tasked with damage control. He asked what was wrong with the letter and how they could "fix" this.

I wanted to know if he had even read my letter and grasped the experiences of our families and the difficulties we faced. I also expressed that their initial communication with us had come several months after losing our son, which seemed very late. Their method of delivery also disrespected every soldier who had ever died for this country. I asked why the condolences from the White House had not been delivered by the brave Marines that Joey had served with and who had accompanied him back to American soil following his death.

Every day, the military and Washington receive a report on casualties, including the names and dates of death of each soldier. It took over a week for our Fallen Six to return home, yet the Marines came to our home the same night. They knew! The Marine Corps had done everything possible to honor a Fallen Warrior. So why not our leaders from Washington?

I got very few answers. Were the politicians too busy? Like his other fallen comrades, Joey loved his country; they all deserved much better. I also inquired about the location of his medals, ribbons, and NCO saber, as we had not yet received them back. The reply was, "I don't know."

It was a futile conversation with mostly unanswered questions. We ended the call. However, twenty minutes later, the commander called back and read me a list of Joey's awards. He said," He was a highly decorated young man."

Really? I thought *as if I didn't already know that.*

Once again, the saying "Too Little, Too Late" applied to all of them. After several conversations with this man, I think he was finally beginning to understand what had to be done. He stated he had placed Joey's photo on his computer's screen saver and looked at it every day. *The New York Times* had posted a stunning article called "The Faces of Dead," and every soldier killed in this conflict was pictured. What a grim reminder of what war does.

I asked the commander to look at those young men in the article and to share it with anyone who should care. I inquired if the President had seen my letter, but he remained silent. I asked the commander if he worked in the White House, and he replied, "Yes."

"Well, take it down the hall and give it to him," I urged. But again, there was nothing but silence on the phone.

Shortly after my last conversation with him, I received a call from the office of General James Amos, Commandant of the Marine Corps. When our men came home, this great man attended the Dignified Transfer in Dover, Delaware. However, there was no representative from the White House on that cold, rainy night in January at 4:00 a.m. Why not?

The Lt. Colonel I spoke to was an honorable man who was sincerely dedicated to the Corps and was following orders to address this problem. He had commanded Marines in this war and stated he had lost 17 Marines. He knows the grief and pain of losing a brother.

In my conversation with the Lt. Colonel from General Amos' office, I expressed that my frustration goes beyond just our six men losing their lives. The *reason* for the loss needed to be explained to me. We had received a letter from the Department of the Navy stating this incident was a "terrible accident." What a statement! That did not explain anything.

We believe the cause was a complete mechanical breakdown of a four-decade-old machine. Did the military have any business flying it in combat? Who was responsible for what happened? Men go to war, men die, but equipment should not take their lives.

The Lt. Colonel continued to talk about several other things. And I asked him a critical question: Where were the things that might have made this terrible loss more bearable? I told him that before Joey was taken away to be cremated, our funeral director asked if we wanted his ribbons, buttons, NCO belt, and buckle that he wore so proudly. What a thoughtful man to ask this question. The funeral director had retrieved them for us because we could not view our son. But once again, I asked who should have presented them to us. Many unanswered questions lingered after our call, and there were a lot of "I don't know" answers given in response to our inquiries.

In response to my questions, the next phone call I received was from the commander of the Air Wing in K-Bay, Hawaii. Once again, the call was from an honorable man who asked what could be done. I informed him that I had no intention of causing the problems resulting from my letter.

Can you observe how one part of the system transferred my questions to another and then another without any of them assuming responsibility? All of them thought, *if we do something, then it is all right.*

The entire chain of command had broken down; it was time to be set right. On this call, once again, I brought up the topic of Joey's missing personal property. After eight months, it was discovered during an investigation that Joey knew the individuals who had the items in their homes on base. A huge number of things have gone missing during this entire ordeal. It makes you wonder how many times this has happened, and no one has asked the simple question of "Why?"

90th Floor

ON SEPTEMBER 11TH, 2001, our country was attacked by an evil that still exists today. This act propelled our nation into a never-ending war that has claimed far too many. I remember it well. Our family was on vacation in Branson, Missouri. Joey and I were canoeing and fishing on Lake Taneycomo, which flows through the heart of Branson.

We had just pulled into the boat dock and walked into the bait shop. The TV was on, and several men were gathered around it, watching in disbelief. I asked what was going on, and someone mentioned that terrorists had just bombed the World Trade Center in New York. I thought he was kidding—how could this happen—but it was true.

Everyone was in shock, and I looked at Joey, 12 years old at the time. Who would have thought that seven years later, he would be at war against this evil? Almost all the Marines who served with him were kids at the time. What compelled them to enlist during a time of war?

The towers fell that day, and a new structure was built in the exact location. The One World Trade Center in NY, now stands there, showing the world that we will rebuild and be better than before. This brings me to a Marine named Tom Stivers. On October 17th, 2012, he and his family were taking a tour of the 9/11 museum. Part of the tour was the Freedom Tower, and they ascended to the 90th floor.

As he explained it to me, the floor was not completed. There were no walls or windows, just open spaces to the ground 90 stories below. The only thing preventing anyone from falling was an orange cargo netting fence! The blast wall was still exposed, and the tour guide told everyone they could write anything on the wall. Look up the "090th floor signature wall" on the internet to get a visual feeling of this monument. Tom Stivers wrote the following:

> God Bless America, Never Forget,
> Capt. Dan Bartle,
> Capt. Nathan McHone,
> M.Sgt. Travis Riddick,
> Cpl. John Faircloth,
> Cpl. Jesse Stites,
> Cpl. Kevin Reinhard,
> Cpl. Joseph Logan,
> Sgt. Alex Limjoco,
> HMH 363,
> Lucky Red Lions.

In addition, Tom added, "I love you," to his wife, Donna, and daughter, Aubrey. What a touching ending to one of the noblest gestures I have ever seen. Tom sent me a photo of the wall with all the names on it. Two more photos really brought home what the new building meant. The one taken from ground level was stunning.

Tom stood at the base of the American flagpole, looking up. The flag was unfurled, blowing in the wind. The picture was taken at such an angle that it took in the entire height of the building. It captured the glass windows as they reflected the glowing sunlight. This was a shining image I will always remember.

The last picture was taken from the 90th floor across the bay at the Statue of Liberty. She has been standing there as a symbol of our country's greatness. These photos did my soul good knowing that young men like Tom still believe in the foundation of this country. He fought for her to keep her free. In my parting words to him, I invited him to the mountain so he could sign the Red Lion Wall. Semper Fi, Marine, and thank you again!

The Flag Flown Over Washington

THE DATE WAS October 24, 2013; the place was Arlington National Cemetery. Once again, the families of the Fallen Six gathered to say a final goodbye. This was the Group Burial of the remains of our brave Marines. There were hundreds of people in attendance, mostly military, Marines, and members of the HMH363 RED LIONS, paying their final respects.

It was an honor to see how many people returned for this ceremony. My heart was happy to see them in their dress blues. But I was also so sad about what they all endured during the war. One person stood silently in the crowd. Her name is Mary Beth Gerrity. She is Kevin Reinhard's aunt and Kathleen's sister.

Before the ceremony, we greeted and spoke to several people we had not seen in two years. Mary Beth had been in contact with us throughout this time. This great lady had hand-knitted six beautiful blankets for the beds for the Red Lions Project. They will always be treasured for the memory that they represent.

She also took it upon herself to research for grants that will eventually help fund and build the Project. This speaks highly of her and her caring, loving heart. Thank you for your work, Mary Beth.

But she did one more simply amazing gesture that will always have a lasting impact on me. Mary Beth contacted Congressman Leonard Lance of New Jersey to have a United States flag flown over the Capitol Building in Washington, D.C., in honor of our Marines on that day. It wasn't until the flag arrived at our home that we learned how she had done such an honorable deed.

I opened the box, read the letter, and looked at the certificate within. Mary Beth had made history for six great men who gave their lives for this country. This flag will be flown on Red Lions Mountain with gracious respect from the lady who made it possible.

Thank you, Mary Beth, with all my heart.

Arlington

THE MEMORIAL SERVICE on October 24, 2013, would be the last. It started in Afghanistan on January 19th, 2012. Our Fallen Six would be placed to rest, but only part of them. Daniel Bartle, Nathan McHone, Travis Riddick, Joey Logan, Kevin Reinhard, and Jesse Stites were our Marines. They were brothers in arms, a bond that will never be broken.

Imagine: they lived, ate, slept, worked, laughed, cried, fought, and died together. This is beyond family, above friendship, a bond that only a very few will ever know. The love these men had for each other can only be seen in the ones that have returned from war. These were intense men who had a commitment unmatched by all that knew them. If only our country had this same virtue, we would become great again.

Where do these great men come from? They come from everywhere, every town in America, as did their forefathers. They answered the call of duty that so many have forgotten. They were ordinary men thrown into extraordinary circumstances. They are the unsung Heroes that no one knows about. Now, they will be placed in the ground alongside all who have gone before them.

When the letter came informing us that there would be another service for the men, I was in total shock and disbelief. All six of the families had received two sets of remains of our Fallen Marines. For us, it would be the fourth service we would attend. The wound was torn open again. You could only imagine what had happened to the men during the crash. God only knows why we are going through this repeatedly.

The letter stated that it would be a "Group Burial," with a part of each man buried together for eternity. You don't understand what war really does until you read those words. There were no other words that could be written to change what had happened.

Waiting and preparing for what was to come was the hardest part of this journey. Contact with the military is always done with much confusion and misinformation. All you do is sit and wait for the next call or email. They are not the best at dealing with the emotions that come with each family's needs and requests.

What happened in the past has changed things, and the political pressure keeps them from doing what's right. One stunning example of this was when I asked if Joey's best friend, a Marine who escorted Joey home to Texas for the first time, could be present in Arlington.

The first question was, "Is he immediate family?"

As far as I was concerned, he was his brother. But I was told he could not be paid for. I was brought to tears once again over the response. I called everyone that I thought could help make it happen, but I got the same response.

Who is responsible for making decisions regarding a serviceman's death? You see every day how our military is used and abused by the government, while the politicians go to every kind of event with no concern about the cost. What is the cost of one of these lives given for this country?

Stephen Cassman is the Marine who I am speaking of who came to Arlington to see his best friend buried again. He had to take his own leave, and we had to pay for his room and plane ticket. The true Marines who would help in this matter were the East Tex Marine Corps League, who paid for the plane ticket. I will be forever grateful to these fine Marines for answering the call when our government would not. Semper Fi to all of them, I truly know what those two words mean.

There was a two-month wait before we were given the exact date of the ceremony. October 24th was assigned by the powers that be. This date is also my wife Debi's birthday. What a disturbing event taking place: burying your son again and celebrating another year of life. Life is very unfair sometimes, and this was one of those moments.

We left Houston on the 23rd and would return on the 25th. These three days set me back to the beginning of this tragedy. You almost have your emotions under control, and then it all boils up inside and explodes. Going to Washington, D.C., is an experience I never want to go through again.

What bothers me most is that the politicians who made this war happen do not care who gets hurt. Knowing they were so close to where I was staying gave me a sickening feeling the entire time I was there. I wanted to yell from the hotel to see if they could hear my pain. I could see the White House and Pentagon from the room.

Another example of inconsideration was the lack of help for the Reinhards, Jim and Kathleen, parents of Kevin Reinhard. They were told that they had to make their own arrangements to get to Arlington. The Marines and government would not provide transportation or allow their CACO Officer to attend the service.

They drove themselves from New Jersey to Arlington and would later be reimbursed. It's ironic that we flew in from Houston, and our CACO Officer was allowed to come. Is there no standard for the burial of a Fallen Marine or any Serviceman who died for his country? "Gone, but not forgotten" does not apply.

Grief is a terrible emotion, and to bring it back three times, I will never recover from the memories. The ceremony that we were about to see cannot be written about. You must be part of it to understand. Yes, they are all together in a great place of honor, but why?

We were taken to the cemetery on a Marine bus provided by the base close by. It is a grand monument. If you don't have tears in your eyes, that is. I was so sad, angry, and burning with emotion that I could not believe this was happening again. I burst into tears at the first sight of the white grave markers coming into view. There are thousands of them, 320,000 of them standing row after row. I wish every citizen in this nation would walk through the markers and read the names on the stones. Maybe then, they would understand what it means to be an American.

The bus pulled into the parking lot in front of the chapel. Already assembled, the band was dressed in striking red uniforms. The young Marines who would carry the casket were standing by. These were impressive men, giants, standing at attention alongside the horse-drawn carriage. Marines from all over the world were standing by. These were the friends of our Fallen Six. All branches of our military were there: the Army, Navy, Air Force, and our beloved Marines.

What a gathering that was taking place. Family and friends were filing into the chapel, people I had met, and others who were there to pay their final respects. I was in awe; hundreds were present. As we stood outside, I walked through the crowd, greeting so many familiar faces. I looked at everyone who was there. There was sadness in all their eyes.

Everything was directed to perfection. Army officers escorted the family members into a side entrance, where we were greeted by a lovely lady who talked about what was going to happen. There was some final paperwork to complete. A Marine Lt. Col. and a Sgt. Major, who represented the Marine Corps, and General Amos greeted us. We were handed a card from the General. Looking around the room and seeing all the faces we had seen in Dover, Delaware, it seemed like yesterday. Nothing had changed. The tears still flowed, and the pain was ever-present.

They call this ceremony "Final Closure," but in reality, that will never happen. They gave all the families a book called *Where Valor Rests*. It is the history and pictorial of the cemetery. It is the saddest book ever written. Leafing through the pages pierced my heart. All the lives lost, and every one of them is a story never to be finished. I will never open this book again.

What does this mean when it happens over and over again? War has destroyed so many lives, and all you get in return is a book, flowers, and "I'm sorry." All the "I can't imagine how you feel" statements will never bring them back. If not for my faith, this all means nothing. God has His plan, and this is a great test.

Even during this time of sorrow, the staff had paperwork that they had not completed. The first question was, "Could you circle a symbol of your faith to put on the marker?"

God has no symbol; only He allows them into heaven. Mankind has no clue as to what happens after you pass. I have seen many miracles that only bring my belief to the highest level I can endure. After making this small, feeble attempt to make us feel good, they ushered us into the chapel.

We filed into the front rows of the building, where tens of thousands of caskets had been placed at the altar at one time or another. As fate or some other miracle would have it, I found my seat in the front row, right-hand aisle, next to the altar. The casket was within arm's reach. It took all my strength not to walk over and touch them one more time. Looking back, I should have.

The Chaplain spoke, but I did not hear a word he said. How often does he say the same thing? There was music and singing of a song, but I could not speak. The only thing that was going through my mind was when this was going to stop. *How many times can you bury the same men?* This was the third time.

Finally, the ceremony ended. The Marines moved forward and carried our men out to the carriage. With precision, the casket was placed as the horses stood waiting to move down the road. The order was given, and all that attended walked behind for almost a mile.

I was ahead at first, but my position progressively held back. I talked to some people I knew and others I didn't. I found myself at the rear of the group, walking with Lt. Col. Revor and Sgt. Major Green. They were there from the beginning and were there at the end. I thanked them for attending as we approached the gravesite.

Sikorsky—W.W.N.F.

THIS MEMORY IS special but blurred with the emotions belonging to it. All the families of our Fallen Six were in attendance for the memorial service at K-bay Marine Base in Hawaii. We were attending from different parts of the country, yet all we had in common was that our loved ones had died together in a war. It was not a good time for us or the unit.

The service was held on the flight line, with hundreds present to pay their respects, this time, to the families. Six pictures of our Fallen Marines, along with the Soldier's Cross, were displayed behind the podium for the ceremony. The Soldier's Cross included a helmet, rifle, combat boots, and dog tags dangling down. I watched as every member of the unit went forward, took a knee, and touched the dog tags. This was the second time the families met. The first was at Dover, Delaware, for the Dignified Transfer, when the remains of our Fallen came home to American soil. Now, we were seeing all the men and women who served on the deployment.

The ceremony was intense, with members of the unit coming forward and talking about their fallen friends. I couldn't bring myself to look around, overwhelmed by the sounds of people crying and sobbing. Six members of the unit came forward to speak and give a eulogy about their friend. The Staff Sergeant who spoke for Joey gave him high praise, stating he was the most-flown observer and earned two sets of Combat Air Wings during the deployment. The event was concluded by the Navy Chaplain, and the families were directed to the hangar for a reception to meet the Marines. I walked past a CH-53 sitting on the runway. Its size and power dwarfed me as I pictured Joey and the crew inside.

The hangar was set up nicely, and the Red Lion's commanding officer, Lt. Col. Mark Revor, spoke to the men and the families. Now, it was time to meet the Marines. I had heard stories about some of them when Joey would call home. Now, they were standing there, most not knowing what to say or do.

On a large table lay shadow boxes of our loved ones. Within each box was a picture, medals and ribbons, unit coins, and patches, *another stark reminder that they were not coming home.* Next to each box was a book that was used to sign and write in. Later, I read what members of the unit wrote about Joey. Each family received this book. The shadow boxes were taken and placed on permanent display in the unit's new headquarters in Miramar, California.

These Marines were a family, and their words were sincere and loving as I read the pages in the guest registration book. The most vivid memories were captured in a photo album that rested on the table. It was bound in a desert brown camo fatigue shirt with a green T-shirt showing through the collar area. Each Marine's rank insignia was on the lapels and name tag, and "U.S. Marines" was inscribed above each breast pocket.

Opening the book and looking at the pictures made it seem like I would turn around and see him standing there with that huge smile on his face. It was only a photo book, telling a story of his life during a war. I closed the book and cried again. The tears will never end.

During the reception, I was allowed to speak to the unit and present them with the plaque I had made. It was a round wooden disk with a rich mahogany-colored finish on it. The plaque spanned thirty inches across, with a hub in the center and six bayonets radiating out from around the hub. Six blades on the rotor prop of the helicopter, six men who crewed the bird known as "Iron Tail-06". On each blade was engraved the names of the crew.

Centered at the top of the plaque, carved in bold, gold letters, was "USMC." Below that, was the Eagle, Globe, and Anchor. And further under that, are the words "Semper Fi." At the bottom, centered between the blades, was the date, "01-19-2012, Camp Bastion, Camp Leatherneck, Helmand Province, Afghanistan, HMH 363 Red Lions." This plaque will always be a reminder of six great Marines who gave the ultimate sacrifice.

The plaque was presented to Lt. Col. Revor and viewed by all who were there. I will write about the plaque later, as it deserves its own special place in the Red Lions' history. After that, we all got to meet the members of the unit, and they talked with the families. It was very hard for them, and we understood. What do you say to someone who lost a loved one, and to them, *a fellow Marine?*

Sgt. Spriggs, the group's spokesman, approached Debi and me, carrying what appeared to be a trophy. Several other Marines surrounded him. Their names and faces are very familiar to me now and are in my thoughts daily. The group included Sgt. Combs, Sgt. Stoltenberg, Cpl. O'Sullivan and Sgt. Bobrowski. They were good friends with Joey and have kept in touch with us.

"We took it off a helicopter that was scrapped over in Afghanistan," Sgt. Spriggs said as he handed the piece to me. It was a control foot pedal. According to Sgt. Spriggs, he and O'Sullivan had crafted this in honor of Joey.

They had worked hard to restore it to its original condition. He also said it was covered with dirt, grime, and a rubbery coating and was just nasty overall. *I took his word on that!* Continuing, he said it was from the bird Joey had flown just a month earlier.

In their terms, it was a "hard landing," But in reality, on a mission in a remote area, the helicopter crushed all the landing gear upon impact. Joey had brought it up on one of his calls home. According to Joey, both he and the crew were "grounded" while they investigated the crash. They had all walked away from that one—but not the next.

At that time, I begged Joey to quit flying and stay on the ground; after all, he had only a month left on that deployment. But that hard-headed, loyal kid told me he could not do that because he loved to fly and *would not let the men down.* On their very first flight, after being cleared to fly again, they went down. *God, if only he had listened.*

Looking at the control pedal made me realize how much this group of Marines cared for Joey and the crew. They had transformed a worthless, busted-up foot pedal into a work of art—a symbol of what they stand for. The main body was painted dark green, and "SIKORSKY" was written in bright silver on the top of the pedal.

Attached in the middle was a Lucky Red Lions HMH 363-unit coin with the Red Lion and green shamrock. Down at the bottom was an additional red pedal and a set of Combat Air Wings with three gold stars centered in the middle. And last, at the bottom, was a gold plate with Joey's name engraved on it. This was the most special part of all.

Joseph "Caveman" Logan

"Caveman" was the call sign given to Joey while he was flying. The group of Marines said that he lived up to his name, both in the air and on the ground. Under that name, written in capital letters, was "W.W.N.F."

I paused for a moment, not knowing what this acronym stood for. When they explained the inscription meant "**W**e **W**ill **N**ever **F**orget," it had a profound impact. They gave me the piece in remembrance of a great friend and an even greater Marine.

Semper Fi, Marines, and thank you for your loyalty.

The Lioness in the Darkness

UNDOUBTEDLY, Montana was Joey's favorite place, and he hoped to settle there after leaving the Marines. He called one day and told me he wanted to move to the mountains, build a cabin, find a job, marry a good woman, raise a family, and live a quiet, simple life. I agreed wholeheartedly with his dream. If life had been different for me, I would have done the same.

Joey never made it to Montana, but after he left us, his dream and strong spirit led us to a mountaintop in the Rockies. The search for this special place was long and emotional. Retracing the journey he and I took the summer before he left for the Marines was part of the trip set in front of my wife, Debi, and me. After a month-long search, we found a tract of land in Mineral County, Montana. It was the first gift I call a "miracle." Several miles back on a less-traveled mountain road, nestled in a peaceful setting, was almost as close to heaven as you can get here on Earth.

The land was secured that first year. The second year, we built the first cabin: Joey's cabin. A lot of logs, sweat, and tears went into its construction. I built a memorial there to honor a great son and Marine.

The abundance of wildlife in the mountains is what attracted Joey to the wilderness. Mountain lions roamed the peaks and valleys between the Montana/Idaho wilderness, which was called the Lolo National Forest. The property that makes up the Red Lion Project is called "Cougar Gulch," and the section directly below it on the mountain is named "Cougar Meadows."

The original pioneers who settled in this region named this area for the numerous cougars around it. I love to observe wildlife, so I set game cameras along the trails and paths that crossed through the mountains.

There's something special about a particular place on the property, located on a high overlook. Here, we laid Joey's marker stone, a gift from the Veterans Administration for his burial site. His ashes are there, and a Texas-size cedar cross marking his belief in Jesus Christ. In the center of the cross is carved a Red Lion. We taught him to believe in God, family, and country, and he loved them all.

One dark night, around midnight, the game camera I positioned there took a photo of a mountain lion. The beast stood in a regal pose, seemingly guarding the site where this young hero rests for eternity. The fact that a Red Lion had been laid to rest in places named "Cougar Gulch" and "Cougar Meadows" surely wasn't just by chance. I believe God has a way of telling us things. Therefore, this location would now be known as "Red Lion Mountain."

Semper Fi, and God bless our Marines.

Over We Go!

November 2013

LOOKING BACK, I realize there were many other wonderful times with my son, not just the experiences we shared when fishing. There's a story from years ago that I believe happened for a meaningful purpose. The situation itself led to this becoming a regular occurrence whenever Joey and a group of his friends got together.

On a fall weekend, Joey and company would hang out and make a bonfire. I remember the glow of the fire coming from the backyard but did not realize how much fun they were having. Naturally, there was some beer involved. There was a standing rule at my house: if you party here, you stay the night. I never participated in the entertainment, but now I know why I didn't.

In the fall of 2012, Jim Reinhardt, father of Cpl. Kevin Reinhardt came down to Texas for a visit. We were deer hunting and just having a good time together. He met some of my redneck friends and did not know how to feel about the down-home hospitality offered in Texas. Jim is from New Jersey, and they do things *a little differently* up there.

One afternoon, I took him over to a friend of mine's place in the "country." Our friend Kathy owns property in our county, away from town, and we hunted there off her back porch. We were sitting in lawn chairs, waiting for the deer to come out of the woods. As it started getting colder, we moved inside, opened the sliding patio door, got comfortable in the recliners, and watched NASCAR on a big-screen TV. Occasionally, we would look outside to see if a deer had shown up yet. After a few Jack Daniels and Coke, I lost interest in deer, but Jim kept looking out the door.

All of a sudden, he cried, "There's a buck!"

"Shoot it, and we'll go pick it up with the golf cart," I told him.

"Really?" he replied, with a surprised look on his face. He steadied the rifle. The shot rang out, and the deer hit the ground. "Is this how you hunt in Texas?" he asked with amazement.

"Yep! And it's perfectly legal!"

We piled into the golf cart and loaded the deer. His first Texas deer was a beautiful 6-point buck. After we processed the deer, we headed back to my house. It was time to relax after a long day of hunting.

When we got home, I informed him of another Texas tradition that came after a hunt: making a bonfire and sitting around swapping stories while drinking beer. Naturally, he was all for that. We piled up the logs, and before long, we had a raging fire.

It felt good to sit there with a friend. Jim and I had been through a lot since our sons died in Afghanistan. My son-in-law, Chuck, came by, and Tommy, my eldest son, was sitting with us. We had a few more beers, and the stories got bigger.

We were sitting on the typical white plastic lawn chairs that everyone uses around a campfire. Then, one of the strangest things happened. Both Jim and I *flipped over backward* in the chairs. We lay there on the ground, stunned, looking at each other. We were on level ground and weren't anywhere close to being drunk enough to fall out of a chair. Chuck and Tommy burst into laughter as they watched us two old guys struggling to stand up.

I said, "It's not that funny; help us up."

Jim asked, "What the hell just happened?"

"Hell, if I know!"

At the same moment, the boys stated, "It was Joey knocking you out of your chair."

Chuck added, "Kevin must be here too!"

Tommy went on to recall a story. "Remember all those bonfire parties that went on around here? Apparently, Joey thought it was funny to wait until his friends got drunk, and then he would knock them out of their chairs."

I could picture him doing that. He was a playful soul, always getting into something. He usually got carried away. If he had the chance, he would mess with you and then laugh until he cried.

Tommy proceeded to explain why there were no additional lawn chairs at our house. After Joey knocked a few of them over, the chairs would break and then be thrown into the fire. It was a smart move, getting rid of the evidence so Dad wouldn't get mad.

Jim listened in disbelief, but there was no other explanation. So, Joey got Dad again, and Kevin was along for the laugh. In life, these two young men had big hearts and personalities bigger than life itself. They will always be with us. This proves it. I believe it, and so should you!

Faith in God

THROUGHOUT THIS entire experience, my faith in God had been shaken. If it were not for the Navy Chaplains who were at Dover, I would be angry forever. Two great men saved me from a complete and total hate that would have destroyed me. These men had the task of helping grieving families who were in shock and had nowhere else to turn.

The first chaplain was P.A. Hyder, a young U.S. Navy Lieutenant. His demeanor and compassion were so comforting; he prayed with us every day we were in Dover. I discovered that he was a Marine, but later felt a calling to become a chaplain. He had left the Corps to do missionary work with his wife. The man went from the Battlefield to the Cross.

Chaplain Hyder said that his mission work was fulfilling, but something was missing. He did a lot of praying, went back into the Navy, and became a military chaplain. He knew what our fighting men needed in the hard times they faced. He was back where he belonged.

War is one of the most terrible things a man can face, and without faith, no one can survive it. The phrase "battlefield conversion" has brought the strongest men to their knees. In the face of adversity, men who have never prayed before now find themselves calling out for God's help.

The second chaplain we met was Commander Charlie Rowley. Being the senior man at Dover, he had a great responsibility and burden placed upon him. At the time, I did not know that he had been assigned 750 Dignified Transfers while he was the commanding officer of the chaplains.

Let me explain what a "Dignified Transfer" is for those who are unfamiliar. When a service member is killed in action, the process starts on the battlefield. Their remains are recovered and preserved to be sent home. They are escorted and flown to Dover AFB. A most solemn ceremony is conducted there to bring the hero back to American soil.

Commander Rowley was there to make it perfect because he fully understood how it affected the families and loved ones of our fallen heroes. The staff at Dover dedicated their lives to that mission. Nineteen heroes came home on the Dignified Transfer flight, which carried Joey's crew members.

We did not know if we would ever see Commander Rowley again, but by some miracle, he came to Texas to conduct Joey's memorial ceremony. What an honor it was to see him again. He told me it was the first and only request from a family he ever received to do a "return home." Our CACO officer put in the request without us knowing. Commander Rowley told us, "I got in a little trouble over it. But it was worth it for him."

You must give the Marines and the Navy their due!

The Red Lion Flag

A CHANCE MEETING at our Fallen Six memorial site in Arlington National Cemetery gave birth to this flag, this symbol. It was January 3rd, and we had just arrived from the airport. We were there to meet our new son-in-law's parents for the first time. Andi, our Marine daughter, and her Marine husband Steven asked if we'd like to visit Joey's grave marker at Arlington Cemetery before going to Steven's parents.

Each time I visit Arlington, an overwhelming, intense feeling takes me to a place where all the souls that rest there are. Tears flow from my eyes uncontrollably. I realize what they went through and how our son's remains, along with those of his crew members, were placed there. Row upon row of markers set perfectly in line.

Steven drove up to the front gate and presented the pass that allowed us entrance as a family of a fallen hero. We proceeded to the site in Section 60. This would be the first time we would see the stone. The four of us got out of the car and walked toward the area that we had previously visited for the Interment Ceremony.

That service stuck hard when we realized only parts of the crew were placed there because they could not be identified. These men did not deserve to go that way. I still remember the last phone call we received from Joey the day he died: "I'll be home soon. I can't wait to go fishing." But later that same night, they were gone.

When we last walked the grounds, there was only bare dirt. But as we approached the area, I was taken aback by the size of the stone marker. It was only right that a monument like that be placed in his memory.

Seeing Joey's name listed first on the top left corner of the stone surprised me. He was always #1 in my book. Once reality set in, the tears came again. By this time, I had stopped asking the question, "Why?" That day, I just looked around and took a deep breath.

The moment was so intense that I did not notice other people walking around us. As I looked up, a woman and a man were standing next to us. They were visiting the marker next to our men. The lady knew I was having a difficult time from the look in my eyes.

I remember saying, "This is our son, Joey, and his crew."

What does a total stranger say at a time like this? Somehow, the conversation flowed naturally, and the Red Lion Project, along with its purpose, became the focus of our discussion. The lady's name was Lisa. She was so understanding; somehow, I can tell that about people. I gave her the Red Lion Project card, and we parted ways.

A few months later, we received a donation from Lisa for the Project. My response was a heartfelt thank you, coupled with a statement that's always been close to my heart.

"I am an American, and I am free today because someone fought, bled, and died in my place. I vow that as long as there is breath in my body, their sacrifice will not be in vain."

This is the truth of our Fallen Six. We hope, in our small way, to help those who come back from war—to show them that someone cares and loves them. We want to give back what was taken from us, a life, and to see the purpose of what they did, making a difference in their lives.

Meeting Lisa in Arlington made me stop and think. To me, it was a miracle, one of many I have received. Looking out over the more than 400,000 sites Arlington holds in its hallowed ground, how did we stand there together at that exact moment? They were visiting the site next to our men.

A chance meeting? I believe not. God has a way of putting people together for a reason.

Somewhere between our meeting and emails, the topic of a Red Lion flag came up. And wouldn't you know it, Lisa is a graphic designer who wanted to volunteer her services. The project needed a symbol. I had looked at many Red Lion drawings and pictures, but one stood out above all the others. It was the Lion that was painted on the nose of their helicopter the night they went down. That had to be the flag!

I called Lisa, and she went to work creating the image that would fly on the Red Lion Mountain. I had a vision of it unfurled in the wind at the highest point on the property. After a few more emails and a long season building on the mountain, Lisa sent me four prints of the Red Lion. The strongest, simplest Lion immediately caught my attention. It was a bright red graphic with an outline of green shamrock around it. The flag was pure white. What a stunning symbol to represent our Fallen Six.

Lisa contacted me again and told me that the print had been sent to a flag company and that the process was underway. I called her, and all I could say was, "Wow!" and I thanked her so much. I thank God each day for the total strangers who come into our lives. They are no longer strangers but have become lifelong friends. She said the flag would be done soon. All I could do was see it in my mind.

The day came on November 19th. This was not a random date; it was another month marking the loss of our heroes. The anticipation of opening the box was hard to imagine. Debi and I took it up to my office, which I call the "War Room." It contains all of Joey's military belongings. It is a very special place where I spend a lot of time.

Stepping into the War Room, you're immediately struck by an overwhelming intensity. Joey's life is on display there. We opened the outer mailbox and found another box bound with a red ribbon inside and with a card attached. The face of the card read "Hello," and inside was a short note from Lisa.

I can't control my emotions or what I say anymore. This was one of the best gifts we have received. Opening and holding the flag at arm's length brought back the memory of Joey giving me his Marine Corps Flag to put on the wall of my office. I look at it every day, remembering the giant smile he had on his face when he gave it to me. Semper Fi, Marine!

That day, I was confident that Joey approved of his new Red Lion Flag. After I composed myself, I put the flag on the flagpole in front of the house. The wind lifted it up, and it flew with honor. It will have a place on the mountain when we return in the spring.

Thank you, Lisa!

An Unexpected Gift

DURING JOEY'S DEPLOYMENT, we received unexpected but always welcomed phone calls at all hours of the day or night. Several times, I answered the phone and was greeted by, "Hey, what's up, Daddy-O?"

My reply would be, "Do you know what time it is here?"

He would say, "I don't really care. I had a few minutes and just wanted to see how everything was going at home." These were some of the best talks we ever had!

One night, he called, and we talked about the hunting and fishing trip we were planning when he got home. The conversation then turned to military equipment and weapons. He spoke about aircrew survival knives and a Benchmade knife he carried. This one was spring assist (in my day, it was called a switchblade).

Joey said it came in handy for cutting things and was quick to use. I asked him if he could send me one, and he quickly said that if he did, he would have to tell them he had lost it and would have to pay $260 to replace it. I told him never mind; I didn't realize the knife was that expensive. Back in the 70s, when I was in the military, we were given K-Bars, and they routinely made it home. Times had changed a lot; I couldn't believe they now had to pay for all their stuff.

We talked for a little longer and said our goodbyes. I forgot about that knife until all his belongings were shipped back from Afghanistan. It was incredibly difficult to take an inventory of all his personal and military possessions. I could not read the paperwork because of the tears in my eyes. Our Casualty Officer helped us go through footlocker after footlocker of all that was left of his life. It was overwhelming seeing and touching every item in the boxes.

I know the Marines in his unit packed all his things. It must have been so hard on them. Only a short time earlier, they were talking and joking around, and next, they received the news of the crew going down; it was a reality.

There, at the bottom of a box wrapped in brown paper, I saw something that looked like a black nylon knife case. I picked it up, and the words "Benchmade—Made in the USA" were on the bottom tag. I opened the case, and there it was—the very knife we talked about. It is one of his possessions that I will always cherish. I take it out of the case every now and then and just smile. It is a special gift.

Understanding The True Value of Treasured Memories

*May there be comfort in knowing that someone special
will never be forgotten.*

A Surprise Thank-You Card

I HAD JUST attended the East-Tex Marine Corps League meeting in Conroe, Texas. Before getting in my truck to leave the event, I noticed a red, white, and blue business card on the driver's side window. I picked it up, and on the front side was an inscription, "Thank You for your service and dedication to our country."

Some handwritten words on the back of the card stated, "I am not certain how to express my gratitude for all you have done to secure my freedom. Please accept this simple card as a small token of my appreciation. A grateful Lithuanian American."

I thought to myself, *who put this on the truck*? I glanced around but didn't spot anyone in the parking lot. Someone knew about the meeting and saw the military stickers honoring Joey on the truck. I figured that somebody from the meeting had done it. I mentioned the situation at the next meeting, which took place a month later. No one knew what I was talking about! I showed them the card with no response.

Fast forward one year. I was regularly volunteering at the H.E.A.R.T.S Museum in Huntsville, TX. This was my regular day to volunteer, and as I walked in the door, Richie Harris asked me to come over and meet someone special. A sweet little old lady named Lilija Grumulaitis stood there and handed me a card.

Much to my astonishment, it happened to be the identical card I had received one year prior. I was taken aback and pleasantly surprised by this serendipitous meeting. The first thing I asked was, "Are you the one who placed this wonderful card on my truck last year?"

Lilija said," Yes!"

I wanted to know the motivation behind her inspiring behavior. She told me that when she was a little girl in Lithuania, she lived during WWII when the Germans were waging war in Europe. She and her family were saved by American soldiers during the war. Later, they were granted permission to immigrate to the U.S., and she became an American citizen.

Lilija Grumulaitis has been thanking every service member she meets. And she attends all the veterans' groups and political functions in her area, thanking them for her freedom. Now, she wants to become involved in the Red Lion Project. What a wonderful lady who loves this country with all her heart. Thank you, Lilija.

The ReNaming of a Bridge

IN 2020 we had the honor of being invited to the dedication of the Wilson Road Bridge in Conroe, Texas, near our hometown. From that time on, the bridge would be known as the Veterans Memorial Bridge. This overpass has a deep emotional memory for our family. After Joey's death on January 19, 2012, in Afghanistan, he was brought home, and our caravan passed under the bridge while thousands of true Patriots stood at attention as the motorcade rolled by.

Seeing our nation's flag proudly displayed on the bridge was an emotional moment. The entire community had rallied together to support us. I can never express my thanks to everyone present on that tremendously sad day. Seeing our friends holding the U.S. and Marine Corps flags on the bridge made me proud of this country and Joey's sacrifice. He and all the great men who have died for this country will always be remembered. This bridge will stand as a symbol for all to see and understand that we are the greatest nation in the world.

Lt. Commander Charles Rowley, the Navy Chaplain who escorted Joey home, had these words to say about the bridge and the people who stood on it that day.

> As I traveled the 57-mile route, the motorcade made its way along the highway and observed thousands of people stopped honoring this Fallen Marine. It took a few moments to comprehend what I was not only witnessing, but was also engaged in. In order to rightly honor this valiant young man, all northbound traffic had been stopped. I was

witnessing one of the most heart-wrenching and compelling events of my life. A few miles down the road, we could see an overpass that crossed the highway. Hanging from it was a large American Flag, and from one end to the other, it was lined with citizens displaying flags. The tears began again. I will always remember this day.

Once again, our family is grateful to everyone who was present on that day to show their love and support. We will never forget all that this community has done for us. May God bless America, and may God bless the people of the great state of Texas.

Two Cigars

THERE IS SOMETHING SPECIAL about a good cigar. The smell when you first open the wrapper and whiff it past your nose is a pleasure to the senses. Clipping the end and tasting the flavor of the tobacco tingles the tongue. Then, light it by drawing the flame into the tip and watching the ember glow. Well—it's a *man thing*. Inhaling the first puff of smoke as it surrounds your face brings a feeling of satisfaction and contentment.

Being around a group of good friends makes it even better. This brings me to the day I opened a special wooden box containing two cigars. I had received the box along with Joey's personal property from Afghanistan. This was a surprise because, on the day of his memorial service here in Texas, I received several photos from Mark Stoltenberg's parents. Mark had sent the pictures all the way from Afghanistan. He and the unit were still deployed, and I will always be grateful for what he did.

One photo showed Joey and Evan O'Sullivan taking a smoke break outside the barracks. The other one was *classic*: five Marines sitting around looking like men with an attitude! Capt. Recalde, Joey, Sgt. Combs, SSgt. Hasset, and Cpl. O'Sullivan were taking a break from the war. The looks on their faces were priceless, with those cigars cocked in the corner of their mouths as they all posed for the portrait. I met these fine men and will always keep the photo in the box with the two cigars.

I will always remember opening the box. The lid had a silhouette of a man on a motorcycle smoking a cigar. Printed on the top was the brand name ACID CIGARS by Drew Estate. I lifted the lid, and a sweet aroma filled my nose.

Down at the bottom were two Kuba Kuba cigars. The only thing that came to mind was that Joey was saving two for when he came home: one for him and one for me. It would have been a fine time to talk with him, blow smoke rings, and drink a few beers. These two cigars are special to me and will never be smoked.

On his birthday, I always smoke two cigars, drink one beer, and then pour a beer for him next to his marker stone and cross up on the mountain. Joey is the one who should be fishing with a cigar and a cold beer in his hand. Thanks for remembering. I will never forget that day.

Love, Dad

Troutaholic Sunday

Sunday, June 23, 2013.

I AM FOREVER GRATEFUL to the many wonderful people who have entered our lives since Joey and his crew team left this earth. Compassionate Americans have replaced the emptiness we often feel with their generosity and empathy. This was certainly the case on a particular day in June 2013.

While Debi and I were working on the Red Lions Project that summer, two men, Kirt Wilson and Martin Kidston of the Missoulian newspaper, contacted us. We had no idea who told them about the project, but they wanted to do a story about Joey and his Marine brothers. We agreed, and the rest was history.

Suddenly, the story was featured on the front page of the Sunday paper. I read it in astonishment! Soon after, people from all over Montana were e-mailing and calling us, which was truly overwhelming. The article presented opportunities beyond our wildest dreams.

One email really touched me in such a way that I had to talk to the man who sent it: Joel Thompson of Montana Troutaholic Outfitters. Considering Joey's passion for fishing and our extensive fishing trip prior to his enlistment in the Marines, I felt compelled to make this call. Just being in Montana, seeing all the fishing adventures there, and knowing how healing it would be for our returning veterans, made this a dream come true.

Joel and I spoke by phone, and he said he wanted to help with the Project. I could not believe my ears; I got a lump in my throat and a tear in my eye. The next thing he said was, "The only way to get to know each other is to go fishing."

The arrangements were made, and a few days later, Joel showed up with a rowboat in tow behind his truck. Before I knew it, we were launching the boat into the stunning Clark Fork River and enjoying a fantastic day on the water, filled with conversations and a bit of fishing. What a great man he is, with a heart and understanding of our veterans.

Joel knew how fishing and the Montana experience could do more good for our recovering Marines than any doctor or group session. I had found someone who shared the same dream and who inspired me to help these veterans for the rest of my life. Thank you, Joel Thompson, for being our official fishing guide. You can find out more about his store by visiting:

www.Montanatroutaholic outfitters.com

Two Owls

IT WAS 06:30, and I had just walked outside to greet the morning—Thanksgiving 2013. I didn't think there was much for me to be grateful for that day. It was not light yet, and the grays and blacks of the night were still there with shadows and images.

As I walked across the yard towards my workshop, I heard the familiar sound of a barn owl. Looking up to where the sound came from, I saw two owls perched there, sitting on the highest branches of a huge old oak tree just past the back fence.

The tree had been dead for many years, and I've been noting each time its branches fall to the ground. Yet on top of its remaining skeleton were these two birds calling in the morning. They were telling me a message that I did not understand.

I see and feel many things now that have helped me better understand life. Lately, I have found it harder to manage my emotions and the daily messages I receive. I hope that one day, they will lead me to my final journey. On that particular Thanksgiving morning, I just stood there and watched and listened. The owl's hoot broke the silence, and I had that familiar sense that someone was nearby.

Spirits are strong around me, and this was one time when I needed some help. The owl is a silent guide. They teach us to trust our instincts and silent impressions when someone's spirit, near and dear to you, is telling you something. The owl's appearance is now alerting me to much spiritual activity around me.

These owls are creatures of the night, symbolizing the darkness within—a place of secrets and treasures I need to tap into. Joey's spirit is around me to help uncover those secrets. The owls appeared to me to heighten my physical and spiritual senses. I can now see and hear things like never before. At times, it's a place of sadness that I have no desire to go to.

However, there is hope and good from all this. The owls are telling me that help and guidance are there for me, but it is up to me to act upon it. It is very hard to make that first step to healing and peace. I know the place and how to get there, but the journey will be long and hard.

This has given me the ability to see into the eyes and souls of others. I frequently find myself regretting the things I observe. This is why I am like I am. There is darkness and light in everyone. I hope to be able to see more light.

I will go about my tasks with timing and skill with the ability to use the strength and power given to me. But pray never to misuse it. True strength is gentle. I am looking for the ability to hear and use the inner voice that comes so softly. I must be thankful for the many gifts that have been given and shown to me. I am grateful for all of them. I only wish I could temper all that is within me to someday give back what I have received.

The two owls have been near me for some time now, calling out their message. This morning, I began to listen to the small voices in my inner thoughts. There will be pain and heartache throughout my life. It must be used for good, and I must be thankful for all that has been sent to me. Happy Thanksgiving to the two owls that brought me another miracle.

Little Big Horn

AN EPIC BATTLE in history took place in the Little Big Horn River basin. I have passed by it several times on the way to the Red Lions Project. The rolling prairie hill and the Big Horn River seem so peaceful now. During our 16,000-mile fishing trip, Joey and I never stopped there. Now, I know why. War does terrible things to a man's soul. After Joey's passing, this place did things to me that pierced my heart.

Debi and I were on our third trip to Montana from Texas. The drive took 2,000 miles and three days. After seeing the road signs on Highway 90 advertising the site, we decided to make a stop. We were on the Crow Indian Reservation as we entered the winding road up to the battlefield. To most, this is a tourist attraction, but for me, it took on a much deeper feeling that overwhelmed my senses.

The sun was shining brightly that day, and the prairie grass was golden with the ever-blowing wind moving it as though they were golden waves. There were no trees up on the site, only down near the river where the cottonwoods line its banks. We got to the top and parked the truck. There were plaques marking different sites explaining the battle. We decided to go to the museum to see what was in there.

It was an old building that smelled from years of standing with little maintenance. Most of the displays were behind glass and consisted of native garments, objects, and weaponry used in the fight. There were weapons used by both sides, mostly period rifles, knives, swords, and ammo found around the skirmish. Several pictures of the Native Americans and troopers were on the walls. Looking at these items gave us a sense of what really happened versus how the books and movies tell the story. It was a brutal place and an even more savage battle.

We exited the museum and walked up the road to the battlefield proper. There were markers scattered all around, surrounded by short, wrought iron fences. Each white stone marker marked the place where a soldier or Native American fell during battle. An intense, incredibly unpleasant feeling came over me as I walked through the markers, reading the names.

It's hard for me to explain how I feel and see the visions, but I do. It's not a gift; it's a curse. I could feel a presence that was hopelessness, agony, and despair because there was no way out except death. It seemed as though their souls were reaching out to me, trying to find the reason why. But in war, there is no reason "Why."

Someone else decides, and you follow orders. A dark emotion filled my soul, and I couldn't help but burst into tears. Debi had seen me in this state before and said, "Let's get out of here."

Every year, when I pass by that place, I remember the lives lost and wish for their peaceful rest.

A Vision from Heaven

ABOUT A YEAR after Joey passed, Debi and I talked about what was to become the Red Lion Project. I was torn between remembering the memories I had and letting the pain subside before starting such an endeavor. I wanted to do something because there was an intense force pushing, driving, and guiding me in an unknown direction. Not knowing if I could handle it, I wanted to show Debi some places that Joey and I fished on our 16,000-mile adventure. So, we decided to start by going to Arkansas on the White River.

The trip there was quiet, with little being said. We had called ahead and made reservations at Gaston's White River Resort in Lakeview, Arkansas. Joey and I stayed there on one occasion when we fished there when he was a kid. Arkansas and Missouri were vacation spots we had taken the family to, so we knew the area fairly well.

Debi liked to go to Branson for the shows and entertainment, especially Dolly Parton's Stampede. Eating chicken dinner without utensils requires some adjustments! Finger-licking good is what you get there! The show is great, with a North-South rivalry as the theme.

Well, we went back to Gaston's to check in. We went up to the desk, and a young man greeted us. We signed in, and the keys were exchanged. Then, the unexpected happened. The clerk said to me, "My name is also Tom Logan."

I looked at him in disbelief, but that was his name! What are the chances? We struck up a conversation, and I told him why we were there. He seemed to understand and said he had a brother who was a Marine. People, places, and events happen for a reason in this life. I have been blessed to understand and believe in a greater power guiding us. It's not always what we want or expect, but things have a way of turning out all right.

We went to the room facing out onto the river, which had a back porch overlooking the water. It was flowing swiftly that evening. I sat out there, imagining Joey and me fishing in this exact same place. A tear came to my eye, knowing there would be no more fishing with him on this earth. Debi sat with me and said, "I know how hard it is for you to be here."

I replied, "I know how hard it is for you, too; you're his mom." We hugged each other and gazed out over the river.

The following morning, I woke up early to find the river flowing calmly as usual. It was a great time to cast a fly at a hungry trout. The sun was breaking over the Ozark Mountain ridge that shaded the river, and the water had a magical sparkle about it this morning. The sun's rays peeked through the branches of the trees, casting light and shaded spots on the water. I put on my waders and walked down the path to the water's edge.

Trout were already rising to the morning hatch of bugs. That was a good sign, so I looked through my fly box to find a bug that would match the hatch. I settled on a foam-bodied mayfly. I waded out a short distance and read the water to watch the flow to present a cast where the trout were rising.

After a couple of role casts, I was in the grove where the swift water and still water met. A couple of casts later, I had a 12-inch rainbow trout dancing on my line. It was a great way to start the morning. Landing the fish in short order and releasing it gave me a satisfied feeling. A few more casts and I moved downriver about 100 yards to another promising spot.

This time, I tied a dropper fly below the dry fly. It was a gold midge. This worked for fish that would not come up to hit the dry fly on top. It drifted about a foot underwater and was very productive. Casting a double fly setup takes a little practice, and on the third cast, I had it where I wanted it. The dry fly on top acted as a strike indicator, and when it went under, you had a fish. As if it had been planned, down went the dry, and it was fish on!

Something was very different this time. There was no familiar flash of the rainbow colors in the water. I thought the sun was playing tricks on my eyes. As the fish pulled the line off the reel, I could see glimpses of gold darting downstream. What was it? I started to gain line, and the familiar shape emerged from the deep pool. It was a golden trout, a rare species that only happens with a generic crossbreed of rainbow trout. I thought to myself, *don't lose this one!* But no one would believe me, anyway.

The closer the fish got, the more excited I got. The leader line was almost into the rod tip. It was net time. With a gentle swoop, the trophy was in hand. What a rush!!!

In my lifetime, some of the greatest moments have been spent alone and admiring what nature has given me. This was one of them. This was the fish of a lifetime. I know it was a gift and know who sent it. As luck would have it, a young man and woman came by in a canoe, saw the fish, and paddled over to admire it. The fellow said, "Are you going to get it mounted?"

I replied, "No. Going to release it. It was a gift."

These days, I fish alone. Not having your son and friends around to discuss the amazing nature of sightings together changes everything. That afternoon, I went back to the place where Joey had caught his big brown trout. The memory was so clear that I felt compelled to go back and relive it. I told Debi where I was going and got into the truck to drive several miles to the spot.

The Arkansas mountain roads winding endlessly around the countryside reminded me why I was here. I could feel a presence with me that seemed like it was always there. It was a yearning to go back in time. I arrived at the campsite below the dam and parked the truck. I planned on fishing but could not make myself grab the rod.

A surprise awaited me as I approached the water's edge. There was a young man with his back to me in midstream casting a fly in the exact spot Joey caught his trout. I thought to myself, *is this real, or am I imagining it?* I turned and walked away with a smile on my face.

The Rose Garden

ONE PARTICULARLY CLOUDY, rainy, and dreary day, while in Missoula, Montana, I felt led to visit the Memorial Rose Garden Park. It was almost as if I was being guided there by an angel—*that happens a lot these days*. People typically avoid parks on days like this when the weather is so poor. But my spirits needed a lift, and I felt compelled to head there.

The Memorial Rose Garden Park was established in 1946 as a memorial to the Missoula-area casualties of war. Originally, the park was developed to honor those who had fallen from WWII. Today, the park has expanded to recognize those who perished in wars beyond WWII, including the Vietnam, Persian Gulf, and Korean Wars. Both the American and Montana flags are displayed and lit 24 hours a day, symbolizing the enduring honor of those who gave their lives for our country.

Over six hundred rose bushes are planted there as a living memorial; the garden includes every species of rose imaginable. On a clear day, the park is breathtaking. However, even on this dreary day, I was confident a trip to the park would bring me solace.

The same reasons that led me to Montana and inspired the Red Lions Project were the same reasons I walked through this quiet park. While contemplating the tremendous loss of my son, I came across a stunning bronze and stone sculpture located in the Vietnam War section of the park. The statue is of an angel lifting a soldier up to heaven and was erected for the 25th anniversary of Memorial Rose Garden Park. There it stood right before me, and all I could think of was Joey and his crew members.

The vision of them being raised to heaven after the crash pierced my heart. I sat on the bench a few feet away from this site, crying and shivering. The cold, damp air cut right through me. It was so hard to regain my senses.

Once my eyes cleared, I began studying the intense detail of the monument. As I neared the statue again, I touched the soldier being held by the angel. Both the soldier and the angel had a peaceful look on their faces. In contrast to my experience that day, they weren't going through pain or getting older.

Grief is a profound experience and a powerful force that cannot be controlled. It teaches you so much about yourself. I can't help but wish my situation had a better, more positive outcome. You don't overcome grief; you learn to carry it with you as you continue your journey.

By that time, the monument's patina had turned green, which made me realize another sad thing about mankind: There will always be war, no matter what is done to prevent it. Man's evilness has existed from the beginning and will remain until the end of time. What hurts me the most are all the great people who have fallen in battle.

Angel of the Fallen - Missoula, MT

Our six Marines and the lives they could have lived were taken in an instant for no reason. This angel and soldier statue will always burn in my heart, along with the memory of our Fallen Six.

Two Pictures, Two Thousand Words

EVERYONE HAS HEARD the old saying, "A picture is worth a thousand words." Two photos shook me to the very foundation of my soul. Let me explain "Heaven's Gate" first, and then the pieces will start falling into place.

Shortly after Joey's death, I was led by an amazingly powerful force that I could not ignore. It became stronger and often overwhelming. I was searching for a place to find peace and fulfill Joey's dream. He wanted to find a spot in the wilderness to build a cabin so all his Marine buddies could enjoy and see what he loved.

Initially, I battled with this feeling. I did not want to retrace all the places we had visited, fished, and explored during the summer of 2008 before he went into the Marine Corps. These were great times, spending a small segment of time with a great kid who soon became an outstanding young man. He and I were of the same mindset, doing things others only dreamed of.

I later found out that he would surpass me in every aspect of life. I was so very proud of him and wished we had been given more time together. God had a better plan for him, and I will have to live with that until we meet again.

The search for that perfect piece of land led back to Montana, near the small town of Superior. Once I set foot on the land, an overwhelming feeling of peace came over me and thus began the Red Lion Project.

The intensity of the feelings led to Joey's headstone and some of his ashes being taken on the journey to be placed on the mountaintop. This place was named "Heaven's Gate" and is a spot where his stone lays facing west into the sunset each day. In the morning, the clouds rest on the top of the mountain, and as the sun warms the earth, they rise, reaching into the heavens. At night, the stars appear to come down and touch the same spot, waiting for the morning dawn.

This is what I see in my dreams and the place where his dream has been laid to rest. The quietness up there is soothing; all you hear is your heartbeat and the gentle breezes whistling through the pine trees.

The time came to place his stone on the highest point on the mountain. We drove the truck up the winding, rocky road, and I opened the tailgate. There was the gray granite stone with his name chiseled into it. The reality of it, *of everything*, struck hard, heavy, and cold as the stone was. He was gone. All that was left was this rock and ashes on a lonely mountaintop in Montana.

The spot was cleared, and the little vial that contained his ashes was poured on the bare ground. I lifted the 100-something-pound stone from the truck bed; the weight felt as heavy as my heart. I carried it several yards and placed it as gently as I could.

It was done. It was set where I wished we could be standing together, looking out over the horizon, wondering what was on the other side. I know that one day, I will know what's out there.

Walking back to the truck, I saw the red cedar wood cross in the bed, which would be used to designate the site. I reached for the posthole digger and went back to dig the hole for the cross. The ground was very rocky and as I dug, tears fell to the ground. I finished the hole, and it seemed that it had drained all my strength.

I went back to admire the polished cross reflecting the sun's rays. It was four feet long and three feet across. In the center, there was a red lion carved with black outlines. This was the last symbol that was painted on the helicopters in his unit in Afghanistan. I reached in and placed it over my shoulder. *It's almost ironic that the weight and burdens of life take you back to the cross*. I slid it into the hole gently as it bottomed out with a thud. It was sitting at an angle with the back side resting on the far side of the hole.

I stepped back to look at what had just been done. I pulled my camera from my pocket, took a few pictures, then sat down next to the cross and cried. It was enough for one day. I left, driving away, looking in the rearview mirror. It seemed like a bad dream that played over and over in my head, only it was real. I came back the next day and uprighted the cross. It was finished.

The rest of the summer went by quickly, and before I knew it, September 6th came along: Joey's birthday. Up the mountain, I went with two beers and two cigars. This is a ceremony the Marines have to honor one of their Fallen. I was about to celebrate this date and remember his life. Drink one and pour one. Smoke one, light one, and place it on his stone. I toasted a great Hero and an even greater son. I knew he was with me that day because he loved to drink beer with his fellow Marines.

Those who knew him placed coins, including quarters, dimes, nickels, and pennies, on his stone. There is a collection of coins up there now. It was time to say goodbye to the mountain for the winter, and I would return in the spring to build the first cabin.

After returning home to Texas, several friends wanted to see pictures of the mountain and Montana. One friend, Josh Hawkins, a former Army Ranger who served three tours in Iraq, looked at all the photos. He knew all too well what war was. After talking for a while, he said his uncle, Gene Parsons, was an artist who painted landscapes. I went over to Josh's house, and he showed me the paintings that his uncle had given him.

They were beautiful and very detailed, almost like looking out through a picture window. Josh had been particularly taken by the picture of the cross and headstone. He wore a bracelet with the name of a fallen friend, just as I do of Joey. The next thing he said was, "I'll call my uncle and see if he will paint the picture."

What a gracious gesture from one soldier to another. The next thing I knew, the painting was done! Josh went to pick it up near Ft. Worth, Texas.

He brought it back to our local hangout, Guns and Ammo Gun Shop, in Conroe. He wanted to show it off to all who came into the gun shop.

It was stunning to me, capturing the vista that surrounded Joey's site. Josh and I were photographed holding the painting. Both he and I were extremely proud of the painting. You rarely encounter men like Josh and his Uncle Gene.

The artist beautifully captured the vastness of the country. There was a pine tree off to the left of the cross with a yellow ribbon tied around it. Next to that tree was another with the top browning out on it. The horizon and the mountain tops were touched by billowing clouds that passed overhead.

Looking down, lay the marker stone centered in the painting. The cross was tilted in the hole just like I had set it. Random rocks and branches were scattered on the ground. What a masterpiece Gene had painted. This gift was priceless and could not be bought with any sum of money.

We all shed a few tears that day. In the room were veterans from several wars. I asked Josh if he would give me Gene's phone number so I could thank him personally.

Gene is an older gentleman who now lives in an assisted living community. He paints to pass the time and loves looking at photos to inspire him. His old eyes and hands can truly tell a story on canvas.

When I called and told him who I was, you could hear the emotion in his voice. He said it was an honor and a pleasure to paint such a special place. This painting had true meaning and impacted both our lives.

I laughed when he told me, "You didn't have to have all of them pine trees up there on the mountain. It took me forever to paint a million of them."

I thanked him again and told him it would hang in a special place in my office. I would soon learn how special it was.

And there it went on the wall in my office, which has turned into a war museum. All three of our heroes, Tommy, who is in the Navy; Andi, our second Marine; and Joey, would send their awards, medals, and anything that they thought Dad might want. I'm grateful that they did because it's the only thing I have left to remember Joey by. This room is where I display my pride in these great defenders of our country. My only wish is that our country would rally behind them, treat them as someone special, and welcome them home with open arms.

I've been chronicling the aftermath of Joey's death; it's always on my mind. One morning, after a restless night, I went up to the office with my camera. My mornings are often filled with a mix of emotions and impulsive moments. Something told me to write about the painting. The painting has a presence when you walk into the room.

There is also a pencil drawing by Mike Reagan, a dedicated artist, a Marine, and a great man. At the time he drew Joey's portrait, he had already done over 3000 and given them to the families of the fallen. Mike draws from 4:30 a.m. until late in the afternoon. The man is totally possessed with honoring the heroes of our nation.

I called him one day to express my gratitude for the picture. He was a humble man and thanked me for raising a great son. He said he was about to be taking requests from foreign soldier's families who lost loved ones in these wars. I am extremely grateful to Mike.

I placed the Montana painting next to Joey's portrait so they could face each other; both were in the left corner of the room. To me, they belonged together and will someday be in the cabin on the mountain. I often go up to my office and just sit and look at all that surrounds me. When emotions overwhelm, it can feel like coming alive. I can only imagine what these young service members went through to earn all that fills this room.

I felt motivated to take some pictures of the room, so I stood up, adjusted the camera, and captured three shots. Then, I viewed them to see how they came out. The first two were normal, but the third one almost knocked me to my knees!

The image of me standing there, quivering, is etched in my memory. In the center of the third photo, a white, angelic, ghostly face hovered over the cross and headstone. It was like someone repainted the picture and placed it there.

How could this be? Why did it happen, and for what reason? Miracles have a way of doing that. I didn't know whether to pray, cry, or simply believe what had just happened. It could not have been a reflection; the painting in the frame did not have glass over it. I went up to the painting, touched it, and tried to see what caused the spirit. Once I calmed down, I inserted the memory card into my computer for a larger view of the third image.

It was there, clearer and bigger. I gazed at it with tears streaming down my face. The next thing was to print a copy of both pictures. I did not want to lose this small moment in time.

Both copies came out, and the image of my miracle was framed in the office next to the painting. I perceive this as a symbol of reassurance that everything will be okay, and I desire my journey to be as tranquil as viewing a painting.

Veteran's Day

THIS DAY started early for me at 5:00 AM. I'm not sure if it was because today was Veterans Day or because I had a feeling something special was going to occur today!

I drove from our little town of Willis to the neighboring downtown Conroe and headed to my local hangout, the Guns and Ammo store. This is a place where locals meet, and because of the characters who visit there, it is always a source of live entertainment. We laugh, talk, and get rowdy. It's a man cave in the truest sense.

Today was different. I turned off of I-45 onto Hwy 105, heading east. There is the Fallen Heroes Memorial Park in front of the county tax office. American flags were positioned near each granite marker, inscribed with the names of our fallen soldiers. Joey's name and three others were on the Afghanistan marker.

After parking the truck in the lot, I walked to the site of the Afghanistan memorial. Looking at all the names overwhelmed me.

As I looked at the monument, I observed a difference in Joey's marker. It looked like flowers! I took a second look, and indeed, there was a display of lovely red, white, and blue flowers on his marker.

What also astounded me was that next to the flowers was a photo of U.S. Marine Steve Cassman, Joey's best friend, and U.S. Navy man Tommy Logan, Joey's oldest brother. The picture was taken at Arlington National Cemetery on October 24, 2013. These men had been photographed while standing next to the coffin that contained the remains of the Fallen Six, who died when their helicopter crashed on January 19, 2012.

I just stood there looking at the marker. Who had placed these gifts there? I had no idea. By this time, I was crying, remembering all that had happened. I was alone, experiencing this little miracle. It seems I'm always alone when things like this happen.

There were benches behind me to sit on, and boy, did I need to sit down for a moment. The USMC bench was directly behind me, and I sat there in a state of emotions, trying to think of who would have known about that photo. I knew it had to be someone local, close by, to visit here.

The photo had been posted on my Facebook page and the Red Lions Project website, and hundreds had seen it. This was like a dream, and I was drawn into it. Time went by, and I noticed an old man walking up to the monument. He had a gray beard and a Vietnam hat on. He sat down next to me; he could see I was upset. I told him what had happened to Joey, and he replied, "I'm so sorry for your loss."

I said, "I am too."

He patted me on the back, and I thanked him for his consideration. He stated he was a member of the local VFW in Conroe. I told him I was, too. Looking at him, I asked if there was going to be a ceremony at the VFW today. He said, "Yes, there is."

It made me wonder why I had not been invited, and I asked the man sitting next to me, but he had no answer. The VFW had supported me when Joey first died, but I hadn't had contact with them in a long while. Had they forgotten me, or did they not want to remember?

I got up to leave as he said, "Goodbye." I still could not figure out who had done this wonderful little deed that I had stumbled upon. I left the park and headed over to the gun shop.

At the shop, a retired Marine Gunny Sgt. greeted me. He always hangs out there, and I told him what had happened. He said, "See, people still care, and that proves it."

"But who could have done it?" I replied.

"It doesn't matter. Someone knows Joey and about what he did for this country," he said.

I started to understand now. Life presents us with numerous mysteries and incomprehensible occurrences that we must simply acknowledge.

The Sergeant and I chatted for a bit before the usual group arrived at the shop just before lunchtime. The regulars loaded up in the trucks, and we headed to eat "Mexican Monday," a little tradition of ours. We ate, laughed, and enjoyed the meal together. Afterward, it was time to head home and take in all that had happened.

After arriving at the house, I received a phone call from Steve Cassman's mom, Andrea. She partially raised Joey when the boys were growing up. She told me she had placed the flowers and the photo there. Finding out that she was the one behind this beautiful gesture made me extremely happy. She told me she visits there often and thinks about Joey and his big grin. I told her I did, too.

We both miss him greatly and would do anything to have him with us again. She felt like she had lost a son, even though he was still serving in the Marines. Neither of us knew that an injury would cause her son Steve to take medical leave within the next year. I hope to see him in Montana on Logan Mountain, drinking a few cold ones in honor of his best friend, Joey.

Another unexpected surprise came in the form of a phone message I received later in the day from a man that I hardly knew who had become like family to me following Joey's death. Dennis Brown, the Conroe Outlet Mall manager, installed an 80-foot-tall LED picture of Joey upon his final return home. To tell a part of the story will make it easier to understand.

The entire community got word that Joey had lost his life in the war and rallied around our family for the support we so badly needed. It was a long procession from George Bush Intercontinental Airport to Willis, TX. The motorcade traveled 57 miles and passed by our house so that Joey could come *home*. The funeral car carrying him stopped in front of the house. Three hundred motorcycles from a Patriot group were led the way.

Dennis's contribution was an incredible and unbelievable tribute to honor the memory of this remarkable young man. Dennis arranged for the colossal picture to be displayed at the exact moment the lead car, carrying Joey, passed by the mall. I looked up, and there he was, bigger than life, looking down on his homecoming. Naturally, this was not the welcome home that a hero's loved ones had hoped for.

The picture was there, a constant reminder of the cause for which Joey had lost his life. The picture stayed on display for three days. Ever since then, Dennis has displayed Joey's image and those of the local men and women who have fought for their country.

Dennis and I often sit and visit and speak about this country and the path it has taken. His son Josh is in the Army Special Forces and has served several deployments. Fortunately, Dennis' son has come home each time unharmed. God and his guardian angel are watching over him.

Dennis's text message arrived at the perfect moment on this specific Veteran's Day. When I was in the gun shop, my phone screen brightened with a message showing a picture of Joey standing in his helicopter, pointing at his first combat mission flag. What a grin he had on his face. How proud he looked standing there after that mission! He was beaming; the flag and this country meant everything to him. He was a MARINE.

The message that Dennis wrote under it said, "As long as I have anything to say about it, Joey will always be on that LED. This is the very least we can do. Thank you, Semper Fi, and God Bless."

Thank you, Dennis!

Ruger Red Lion Pistol

IT HAS BEEN over two years since we said goodbye to our Fallen Six. I got a voice message on my phone. It was from Mark Stoltenberg, a good friend of Joey and a great Marine. He is out of the Corps and attending college in Austin, Texas.

The message was a surprise, and I felt good knowing that his friends cared a lot for each other. This is a brotherhood that few men share. Mark said he wanted to come to the house and visit. He had a little something to give us. I called back right away and asked when he wanted to visit. He asked, "How about tomorrow?"

I told him, "Absolutely, I'll be waiting."

It's about a three-hour drive from Austin to Willis. He showed up at 0900, and it was like greeting another son. I was so happy to see him. We had a lot of catching up to do and only one day to do it. To say the least, his visit overwhelmed me.

The gift he had for us was another surprise. He came in with two Red Lion beer mugs with koozies in them. The mugs had HMH 363 RED LIONS and the names of our brave Marines. Also on the cup was the 4th Annual Onesie Pub Crawl. I asked what that was, and he said you really don't want to know.

In reality, it was a party celebrating the Fallen Six and the memories they left us with. Inside the cup was a donation check for the Project. I was stunned, and the only words that came out were, "Thank you." The party was sponsored by Viet Tran, one of the Red Lions pilots, and Jeesong YI, a close friend of Viet. These parties have been going on and will continue six times, one for each of the families of our men. What an amazing gesture, and we didn't even know they were doing this.

The day with Mark was winding down, and he said he had one more thing to give me. He went back to his truck and brought out a briefcase. Once opened, there was a Ruger 45 auto pistol. Mark had bought it on their first deployment to Afghanistan with Joey. He said he got two, one for him and one for his father. He handed it to me.

Another tear ran down my face. For him to give it to me was one of the best gifts I had ever received. I thanked him again and told him pay backs are hell; expect to get something in return. Mark said, "Don't shoot it until we can fire it together on Red Lion Mountain."

I was looking forward to that day. But sadly, Mark passed away unexpectedly from an illness. We will never fire the pistol together on the mountain.

Thanks, Mark, for being Joey's friend and remembering his family.

Semper Fi, my friend.

Six Coffee Mugs

A WONDERFUL FAMILY contacted me after learning about us through the Red Lions Project website. This was a gift from heaven.

Sonya and Mathew are the proud parents of some great children. Their kids are Brett, Caleb, Carson, Colby, and Carissa, ages 14, 12, 11, 9, and 8, respectively.

Sonya said, "I truly believe that the way we learned about you was simply from God."

I replied, "I believe this, too, because I have been blessed with a lot of miracles in the last three years."

The beautiful letter that Sonya sent is featured below and explains what happened. She wrote:

> I was on Facebook one day, and for some reason, the *Red Lions Project* showed up on my newsfeed. I clicked on the page and started reading. I immediately joined the group and started seeing updates periodically in my newsfeed. Your story touched me, and I began praying for a group of people that I'd never met and never expected to meet.
>
> When Veteran's Day came around, I encouraged my children to participate in our school district program. They each wrote an essay about why they appreciated Veterans and were invited to join other students from our area to place flags at the grave sites at Houston National Veterans Cemetery. But this year, I felt called to do a little more. I talked with God about what He wanted us to do as a family...some way to give something back to those who served our country. And God answered.

He said to have the kids make something for the Red Lions Project. I thought over some ideas, and the image came to mind of soldiers sitting in Montana on a cold, quiet evening, sipping coffee out of a mug with a special message on it. I talked to Caleb, my 12-year-old, and asked him to Google and research "The Red Lions Project" and be ready to report to the family at dinner that night.

During dinner, Caleb told the others what he had learned, the mission of the project, and its meaning. I told him about the idea of making coffee mugs to send to Montana. We decided to paint a lion using finger paints and write scriptures and encouraging words. The kids were thrilled, and we got to work!

That's when I decided to try sending a Facebook message directly to the page. When you guys wrote back and included a phone number, I realized it was a local number! I never dreamed you were in Texas...much less just minutes away. God sure is amazing.

So, not only did the kids have the opportunity to get together and paint the mugs, but they also had the blessing of being able to meet you both and see a Facebook story come to life. They were able to get a little taste of giving a tiny bit back to those who have given so much. It was truly an honor for our family. I don't exactly know why God called us to become a part of this, but I'm so grateful He did and can't wait to see what other plans He has for us.

After reading Sonya's letter, meeting this family, and receiving the coffee mugs as a gift, you can be sure they will someday visit Red Lion Mountain.

Thanks, and God bless.

The Miraculous Yellow Rose

THE BIRTH of a child is an amazing miracle. And the miracle of Joey Logan's birth almost didn't happen. Humans think they know how others should live and what choices they should make.

There was a doctor who told us to abort Joey because, according to his calculations, he believed this baby would be mentally and physically deformed. In this situation, we were aware of the exact moment of conception and would never consider harming an unborn child. This time, believing that we were 100 percent right would save a life and bring new hope into the world.

And as expected, Joey was born a healthy baby with a full head of hair and a big nose. Even at birth, he looked like a grown man. And he brought hope into our world because he grew up into one of the finest young men you could ever meet.

This brings me to the rose garden at our home, which I look at daily. It's outside the kitchen window, and each morning, with my first cup of coffee, a miracle appears. A rose bush was planted for each of our five children after they were born. Joey's was a yellow rose, fitting for how he came into the world, strong and proud.

Miraculously, since his passing, this rose bush has been producing flowers on special days connected to his life. I believe that there is a reason this keeps happening. We are all joined for a reason. The people and events that are placed into our lives—good or bad—are all sent from a higher place. That's where our faith comes into play, and the connection we have with our loved ones is never broken. Certain individuals can see and feel when others lose their sight.

On February 18th, 2012, exactly one month after Joey's passing, I discovered two yellow rose buds on the bushes outside our home. This was an unusual site because roses rarely bloom at that time of the year. Debi was out of town, but I walked outside and touched one bloom that had sprung up from out of nowhere. Instantly, the bloom fell into petals on the ground. I counted 22 petals as I stooped to collect them. Interestingly, Joey was 22 years old at the time of his death.

The next morning, I touched the second small bud that had appeared, and once again, all the petals fell off of it. The second bud had exactly 22 fallen petals. Later, when I mentioned what had happened to Debi, she reassured me that this was Joey's way of telling us he was okay.

Another time, on January 18, 2016, one yellow rose bloomed. Again, this was on the anniversary of the date Joey and his crew members passed away. To clarify the date, it was January 19 in Afghanistan, but the Marines came to our door at 10:30 p.m. on the night of the 18th. That knock on the door becomes an everlasting memory in your heart.

The yellow rose blooming on the anniversary of Joey's death in 2016 was distinct. The rose came from a fresh shoot at the bottom of the bush. In the past, all other flowers bloomed from the top of the bush. Yet, a plant that had been around for 26 years now sprouted new growth.

What did this signal? Hopefully, it is a new beginning and direction in my life. A divine message prompted me to find joy again and embrace peace. I know Joey is with me, and I believe these miracles will provide hope until we meet again.

The Soldier's Cross

MY PURPOSE in Montana is to fulfill Joey's dream of constructing a cabin in the mountains where his fellow Marine warriors can find solace and heal. When he told me about his dream, he assured me he would be on the mountain with them. And, even now, I *know* he is up there, watching over his final dream.

The University of Montana at Missoula dedicated a monument in 2011 that I saw one day on the Internet. At the time, I was touched by the bronze memorial honoring the Fallen from Montana. The war was raging, and my son was in the middle of it.

Little did I know that in 2012, Joey and his crew would have this same cross placed for them in Afghanistan. On October 8th, 2013, one day after my 60th birthday, I was standing in front of this same symbol. This was another miracle that changed my life.

As I stood there in the rain, looking at the people it represented, I saw my family's faces and all who have walked to a site like this. I thought of the individuals who were inspired to build this everlasting memorial and place it here. The hearts and souls that it will touch cannot be counted.

The three-dimensional detail kept my eyes busy inspecting every aspect that it encompassed. The Soldier's Cross looked so real, from the helmet with goggles and chin strap all the way down to the rifle's buttstock. The dog tags dangled down, just like the ones I wear around my neck. Looking at the rifle, knowing what it causes, *death*, made me hear the gunshots that were so familiar to me when I served my country.

The boots struck me with a particular intensity because I wear Joey's own boots that were sent home, the very same ones that walked the battlefields where he fell. The deep pain struck me and cannot ever be removed. I just ask God each moment of every day to help me understand.

Flying High with Nike Air

DID YOU EVER learn more about a person after they have passed than when they were alive? There are a lot of revelations - some serious, some funny, and some best left alone. You wish that you could have spent more time with them to really understand who they had become. This is the case with Joey.

He was an A-type personality, always pushing the envelope for the next thrill or adventure. As parents, we taught him to be independent and outgoing and confront challenges head-on. I did not realize how far he had taken this advice until I looked at several photos of him when he was in the Marines. For sure, the Corps maximized his confidence both physically and mentally.

When all his personal belongings came home from Afghanistan and Hawaii, the transformation of my young man was truly revealed. Picture after picture showed how much he enjoyed every moment of his life. I am very thankful to one of his Marine friends, Mark, who sent us several photos of him taken in Afghanistan. These would be the only surviving pictures from the war.

I know Joey had taken a lot of pictures over there, but his laptop and phone were wiped clean of all that information. The amazing part is that these pictures were all sent while Mark and the unit were still in Afghanistan! And the more amazing fact is that he sent them to his parents here in Texas.

Craig and Camille traveled from Austin, Texas, and gave me the pictures at Joey's visitation in Willis. What an outstanding gesture for them to give us an everlasting gift of remembrance. I had to put this entry into the book because it leads me to Joey and the friends with whom he shared his adventures with the Marines, which brings me to the white Nike Air shoes.

It started on the north shore of Oahu, Hawaii, when a group of Marines and Sailors were celebrating Nick's birthday. Though Nick was in the Navy, Joey had the same job, and they worked together on occasion. They became close friends, and Nick gave Joey the moniker "Boomhauer" after one of the characters from the cartoon *King of the Hill*.

Boomhauer would appear once Joey had several beers under his belt, and he would begin to talk like the character. He would mumble and his speech was not understandable, except by Nick. You can see how they got along. Joey needed an interpreter.

Somehow, this ended up leading the group to a skydiving event. I always said he had more balls than brains, and this is one of the many examples. They all made it up from the south end of the island. I know this was probably Joey's idea because flying was his passion. The skydiving company they jumped with provided a photo shoot and video along with the fall from the sky. Joey later called us at home and told us what a blast they had that day.

Years later, I came across the CD in his belongings and popped it into the laptop. I was amazed at the pictures that were captured as he descended to earth. There he was with his huge smile, his face distorted and flattened by the extreme speed he was traveling. Joey was giving the "Shaka" hand sign, which is a traditional gesture in Hawaii, meaning "hang loose" and "awesome!"

As I scrolled through the photos, I saw that those bright white Nike Air shoes looked huge. The shoe stood out against the clear, blue Hawaiian sky, the emerald, green volcanic mountain behind him. I could tell he was laughing all the way down, with no fear and no regrets.

This started a family tradition (except for me). Debi saw the pictures and said, "That's Joey for you. I want to go there when we go back to Hawaii to visit Andi." Joey's younger sister, Andi, is a Marine, and somehow, she was also stationed at K-Bay. Our next trip had already been planned!

Once we got there, Debi, Andi, and I went skydiving. Well, I chickened out! But the girls boarded the plane, flew to 14,000 feet, and jumped out. I was very happy to be on the ground taking pictures as those two tiny specks kept getting bigger and bigger. Then the parachutes opened, and my stomach did a flip. Now I know where our kids get their craziness: From their mother!

As soon as both landed safely on the ground, they told me I had to try it. I replied, "I've had enough cheap thrills in my life, thank you!" I still have Joey's big white Nike Air shoes, and I look at them to remember that he had a great life. Thanks, kid.

Love, Dad

Grandpa Guiseppe Cioci

GUISEPPE CIOCI was my grandfather on the Italian side of the family, Joey's great-grandfather. It's funny how even though the two never met, they were very much alike. I only put this connection together recently after my mother, Sylvia, sent me my grandfather's military records. These documents were from the First World War when Grandpa served in the American armed forces. It was fascinating to me to see how different this country was back then.

Giuseppe had emigrated from Italy around the turn of the century, making upstate New York his home. There was a great influx of Europeans at the time, all coming to America looking for a new beginning. As fate would have it, he was drafted into the U.S. Army when the war began for us.

He was so proud to serve his new country and to become a citizen. His generation helped build this country with a sense of devotion. We should take a lesson from them. He had just left Europe for a new home but was right back there, fighting a war for the country that had just received him.

Even though I'd grown up around him, I never knew he fought in the Great War. He never spoke of it. Looking back, I realized he was troubled by something but did not understand what it was. I remember that he worked himself to the bone in the shoe factory in our hometown of Endicott, New York. The town was founded by the Endicott/Johnson Shoe Company, and it employed the vast majority of the immigrants who lived there.

One thing I'm always reminded of is that his generation lived a hard life, but there was a strong bond among the people in their community. The family gatherings were frequent, and they did not need a reason to party, dance, play games, or enjoy life. The men were men back then. They were strong individuals, both physically *and morally*, and church and worship played an incredibly important part in their lives.

Fishing with Grandpa was one of my favorite memories. He loved the outdoors, and back then, they depended on game and fish as a source of food. After the war, his generation was thrown into the Great Depression. They had to do without and make do with what they had. Unfortunately, we have become a soft society and would not have survived as they did. They made everything back then.

Instead of a backyard with a lawn, there was a garden providing fruits and vegetables for the table. And don't forget the grape vines! They planted and cultivated vines that were brought over from Italy and used them to make their wines. I remember picking the grapes, and my grandpa showed me how to prune and maintain the vines. The wine was good, and they drank plenty of it!

Looking back at his military service made me understand what this old man had gone through during the war. Going over his enlistment and discharge papers, I saw a record of the battles he fought. The words were written in a foreign language: French. It was titled battles, engagements, skirmishes, and expeditions.

On the next line was written:

"Guardian Sector Vosges, Meuse Argonne Offensive with A.E.F in France."

I had to research this information, so I browsed the internet and was overwhelmed by the information that I found. I took in the dozens of old photos of the battles and really came to a better understanding of war and what it does to a man. This "understanding" would forever be burned into my soul after Joey died in Afghanistan. The nature of war never changes, just the details: the countries involved, and the sacrifices made by those who are called to serve.

A feeling of sadness came over me. Grandpa had returned from war but was forever scarred by the memories that he carried with him. At times, I was able to see the anger, rage, and frequent weariness and detachment in him, but I was too young to understand. Now, I see those same symptoms in our soldiers coming back from war.

Sometimes, I find myself asking, "When will we ever learn?" The Bible states that there will always be wars and rumors of war, so is mankind doomed to repeat this tragedy until the end of the world? I certainly hope not.

Before Joey was born, Debi and I talked about a name for him. I asked her if it would be alright if we named him Joseph, the English equivalent of Guiseppe. Daniel was another strong biblical name, and the story of the Lion's Den came to my mind as a great middle name. Who would have known that he would later become a Red Lion and fight the battles that he did?

It seems fitting that the strength in his name would lead to his calling as a warrior, believing in and fighting for a cause. I didn't realize his lineage and upbringing would make him into the man he became. Looking back on his life from childhood until the end, I can only surmise that he was *meant* to do what he did.

It's crazy that our family history is filled with American heroes, and I am only now finding out about them. I've contacted several family members and am compiling a list of all who served this great nation. However, I can only find one, Joey, who gave the ultimate sacrifice for his country, family, and friends.

Joey's 1940 Chevy

SHORTLY AFTER Joey had passed away, I was driving down FM 1097 and noticed an old car at the local Shell gas station. As I drove by, I watched a young man put gas in the car and drive away. I thought to myself that it would be so cool to restore an old car like that. The driver headed on his way, and so did I, never thinking much about it after that.

Well, the next day, my wife Debi and I were driving down the same road, just about a mile from the house. There sat the car on the side of the road with a "For Sale" sign on it. The sight before me was so unbelievable that I mentioned to Debi that this was the car I had told her about the day before.

We turned around and stopped to look at the car. I called the phone number on the windshield, and a man named John Brown answered. I explained that I was waiting outside and wanted to have a conversation with him about the car.

John came out and explained to me that it was a 1940 Chevy Master Deluxe 4-door. *Boy, that was a mouthful.* We talked about the price and how the car was in such good condition for being 72 years old; it still ran and was in good working condition.

During our visit, four additional cars arrived, and people stopped to look at the vehicle. I looked at Debi, and she looked at me and asked, "Do you want it?"

When I replied, "Yes," she said, "You can consider it a gift from Joey, and you can restore it in his honor with the Marine Corps colors."

She continued with some clever ideas, "Use the brilliant blood stripe red that is on their uniform pant legs, along with gold metallic flack paint for the body. The dark blue of their dress jacket and the light blue of their pants will be the colors for the interior. To top it off, use the white dress belt and gold belt buckle across the seats. Display the Eagle, Globe, and Anchor on the trunk so that as you drive away, all can see the USMC in all its glory. " I could only imagine what it would look like.

We will use it for military functions, displays, and meetings. There will be a host of opportunities, such as Memorial Day parades, Marine Corps functions, museum displays, VFW and American Legion events, and, most of all, the Marine Corps League meetings. It would be a symbol of great honor and respect for our fallen Marines.

We have experienced many miracles and have met so many outstanding people in our community who truly love our country and our military. Folks should love them—they are our sons and daughters. Two of our children are now serving our country: our oldest son, Thomas, is in the Navy, and our youngest daughter, Andi, is also a Marine.

God Bless America and Semper Fi to the USMC

The Red Lion Colt .45 Auto Pistol

BEFORE THE last deployment to Afghanistan, the Marine Corps determined that the HMH-363 Lucky Red Lions would be on the "Sundown Mission" and would be disbanded upon completion of that tour of duty. It was a sad time for the unit because it had been established in 1952 as an aerial combat unit. Sixty years of flying and fighting for our country, a history filled with heroic deeds and tales.

The helicopter they flew in was used during Vietnam; imagine the tales it could tell if it could speak. Looking back on the tragic last flight, I can only wish and pray that they had never gone and wish it had been disbanded before it was too late.

Joey loved what he was doing and was the happiest and most focused young man that you could ever imagine. I remember him calling home one day, saying how great it was to be able to fly around in a helicopter, shoot big guns, and get paid for it. He loved the Marines and finally found a cause worth fighting for. Every picture of him that was sent home had a huge smile on his face. *The Few, The Proud, Earned, Not Given*; that was the way he lived his life.

The pistol I mentioned above was to be a "one of a kind," the only one in existence, to honor the Lucky Red Lions Sun Down Mission. I wish I could identify the person who made the decision to partner with Colt for the pistol, as it was a truly historic event. *"Pistol #48"* did not get its start with the rest of the orders placed with the Colt Firearms Company.

Joey was very busy attending three different schools to qualify as an aerial observer. This took him back to the U.S. mainland for several months before the deployment. And so, somehow, he missed ordering his pistol. I believe he would have been interested in it because he always discussed shooting, firearms, hunting, and fishing during his calls home.

However, this special pistol was not mentioned in any of our conversations. When talking to one of his friends after his passing, Joey told him that he was going to buy his dad a pistol for all the great hunting and fishing trips he had taken him on. It was a great feeling to hear this from one of his close friends.

The time came for the last deployment for our "Fallen Six," and when Joey told us they were leaving, my heart sank. There was a bad feeling about this one. No one wants to see their son go off to war. He kept in contact by phone, and we talked about the outdoors and trips we would take together in the future.

Now, after all that had happened, I realized he was trying to tell me he was not coming back this time. The allure of battle and war is not the glory and fighting for a great cause that people think it is. Our young men and women are dying. And the families and loved ones left behind are the ones that suffer the most.

Debi and I have met all the families of the "Fallen Six" and have become very close. We have become part of a bigger family: the U.S. Marine Corps. The bond that these men have is a love for each other that surpasses anything I have ever witnessed.

Our six Marines will be forever joined together, along with the families who lost them. Time passed slowly, and we became close friends with Jim and Kathleen Reinhard, the parents of Kevin Reinhard, who went down with Joey and the crew.

Among all this pain and grief is when I found out about the Colt .45 Auto. One day, Jim called me and asked if I had received Joey's pistol from Colt.

My first response was, "What pistol?"

He said, "The one that the unit ordered for the Red Lions Sundown Mission. You all didn't get one?" He then explained that Kevin had ordered one, but Joey was not around when they made the order.

I asked him how I could get one, and he said it might be too late now. I never take "no" for an answer, so I began my quest for Joey's pistol. If you deal with the military long enough, you will learn that sometimes, getting information is almost impossible. Instead of contacting the unit, I consulted experts and Colt firearms collectors first.

The gun shop involved in the Colt transaction was found, but they were uncooperative and apathetic towards providing any information. I contacted Sgt. Major Mitchell Green, one of the best Marines I've ever encountered. He put me in touch with Chief Warrant Officer 2 John Johnson, who was one of the key people in ordering the pistols.

The following is an e-mail Mr. Johnson sent me regarding the pistol:

> Mr. Logan,
> I am CWO2 John Johnson, WoJo. I was contacted by Sgt. Major Green, and he informed me of your desire to get one of the pistols that had been made for the HMH-363. But first of all, let me start off by saying your son was a great Marine. In the few interactions that I had with him, I was impressed with his drive, work ethic, and smile that never seemed to go away. He and the other Fallen Marines are missed.

For me to read these words made all that had happened vanish for a moment, knowing that Joey had found a home and Marines who loved him. *Semper Fi* sums up all that makes up a Marine.

In the e-mails sent by Green and Johnson, there was a picture of the Red Lions' pistol, *Serial #001*. What an image of the first of only 50 that will ever be produced. I needed to find out who had this pistol.

The history of the Lucky Red Lions will be forever honored as the symbol of the firearm that has served our fighting troops so well. As a matter of fact, my grandfather, Joey's great-grandfather, served in the trenches of Europe in the Great War. As mentioned previously, Joey is named after him—Giuseppe Cioci.

Our entire family has had warriors through every conflict that our country has been involved in since the First World War. The pistol was ordered from the Colt Custom Shop through a very nice lady named Kathleen. She was very helpful and had Joey's name engraved on the side. She stated it would take up to six to eight months to get it. All I could do was wait.

A while later, a phone call came in while we were in Montana working on the Red Lions Project. It was to be a retreat for returning Marines to relax and find peace in their lives. The call was from Kathleen at Colt, who informed us that Joey's pistol was ready to ship.

"That's great news," I told her.

She replied, "You would not believe what happened here at Colt today. Your Governor, Rick Perry, was here touring the plant. He is trying to get Colt to move to Texas."

I said, "That would be great!"

"As Governor Perry toured through the facility, the management brought him into my office. This is where all the cool stuff is!" said Kathleen, who then relayed a story I will never forget.

Kathleen had mentioned to Governor Perry that they had one of his Texas Fallen Marines pistols ready to be shipped to a waiting father.

"The Marine's name is Cpl. Joey D. Logan," Kathleen told Governor Perry.

Governor Perry was amazed when he heard the name. Earlier that year, on Memorial Day, the State of Texas honored 94 Fallen Soldiers and Marines who sacrificed their lives for our country. And Joey was among the fallen.

My wife Debi and I were invited to Austin to receive the honors for our son. When it was our turn, we went forward and met Governor Perry, who presented us with a Texas flag and a document signed by all the Texas legislators. He told us, "We will always remember your son."

Debi replied, "You will, because my husband has something for you."

I gave the governor a picture patch of Joey in his aircrew helmet, sitting next to his machine gun. The patches are to be sewn on vests or jackets to honor Fallen Heroes. Governor Perry took the patch, we shook hands, and he hugged Debi.

Months later, Governor Perry was at Colt, looking at the .45 auto pistol made in Joey's honor. It became an emotional moment for all who were there. Most of the Colt management are Marines. They know what sacrifice is, and giving one's life is the ultimate sacrifice.

Governor Perry picked up the pistol and admired it, looking at Joey's name on the side. Kathleen said a few tears were shed. He laid it down on her desk, and out of his pocket came the picture patch that I had given him. He then took out his phone and took a photo to record this moment. This is one of many miracles that have happened since Joey passed away. Joey's strong spirit will always be near.

Kathleen's call left me feeling very emotional. It came in while I was driving from Missoula to Superior. After hearing a story like that, I had to pull over to wipe the tears from my eyes.

But what's even more amazing is that when I arrived back in Superior, I received another phone call. This time, it was from Governor Perry's office, telling me what had happened and that he wanted to talk to me. I replied, "Absolutely!" and was put on his call list. Timing is everything, and I waited for the call.

One day after we returned to Texas, my phone rang, showing 'RESTRICTED' on the caller ID. I knew it was Governor Perry calling, so I answered by greeting him. "Hello, Gov. Perry. How are you doing? I understand you had quite an experience at Colt."

"Yes, I did," he replied, "And it was a miracle. What are the chances of me being there, the pistol being there, and its shipping that day?"

"Yes, I understand", I said. "God has a way of telling us things."

He explained everything that happened, and I hung onto every word. "It was a moment in history in which to honor your son and all the Marines who have ever served this great nation."

I told him, "Joey is still with us and will always be there when I need him."

Governor Perry further elaborated on the story. He said when they were at the Dallas airport waiting for his flight, he noticed a display of all the fallen military service members from Texas. He said as soon as he sat down, Joey's picture popped up on the display. He and his staff were in awe of what they had just seen. This young man was strong in life and is stronger now, sending a message to a chosen few. I will spread the word of this miracle and many more that have happened.

The Governor asked if there was anything that he could do for us. I had only one request: to bring the pistol to the State Capitol building and have a picture taken with my wife, the Governor, and myself. He agreed and immediately gave me his Chief Aid's contact number so I could set up the appointment.

This has meant a lot to our family, friends, and all the Marines we have met in the year and a half since Joey died. Governor Rick Perry is a great man, and he proved it by simply carrying Joey's patch. Only God could have made this happen, and I thank him every day for his blessings.

THURSDAY, AUGUST 1ST, 1:00 P.M., THE STATE CAPITOL BUILDING, AUSTIN, TX

What a day this was! Debi and I woke up early for the drive to Austin. Today, we were going to meet Governor Rick Perry in his office. We were bringing the Red Lions Colt .45 Auto Pistol, that the Governor had seen at Colt a month earlier. I couldn't wait to get there.

This was a very special day for us and for the memory of our son, Joey. He earned this visit, and I wish somehow Joey could have shaken hands with

Governor Perry. We are so proud of the accomplishments our son accomplished in his short life. He was one of the few, the proud, the brave Marines who served without question.

We dressed for the occasion, both wearing our bright red Marine Corps shirts with our Gold Star pins. The Governor's staff was waiting for us at the south entrance. I proudly carried the engraved walnut case that enclosed the pistol. The case was carved on the lid with a deep relief and bright gold lettering. The inscription on the box reads:

<blockquote>
Cpl. Joey D. Logan, HMH-363 RED LIONS USMC
Operation Enduring Freedom, Helmand Province, Afghanistan
</blockquote>

At the bottom, Joey's date of birth (09-06-1989) and the date he passed (01-19-2012) are inscribed. On the left side is carved the Red Lion head, and on the right side, the Eagle, Globe, and Anchor. All the engraving is completed in Marine Corps gold.

This box and pistol will be a lasting tribute to one great Marine. The pistol was done up in a traditional military fashion: brushed stainless steel with polished sides. *"SEMPER FIDELIS"* was scribed on the side in bold black lettering.

At the back of the slide, the Red Lion's head was transposed over the outline of Afghanistan. Engraved on the lower receiver frame was *"Corporal Joey D. Logan."* The right side of the slide had a matching Lion head and *"HMH 363, 1952-2012."* The grips had the Eagle, Globe, and Anchor carved in the center on both sides. The receiver was stamped with serial #HMH 363048. The pistol's beauty and simplicity were stunning and perfect.

We went up to the second floor and were taken to Gov. Perry's reception room. The Texas State Capitol building is an awe-inspiring structure. It was built to be the center of a nation, The Republic of Texas. It rivals any capital building in the world. As you walk through the doors, you can feel all the great men throughout Texas' history who have walked through its halls. It is a very humbling feeling. To be invited there was an honor, and the reason to honor our son was even greater.

We were greeted by many members of his staff who were preparing for us to meet the Governor. We were seated for a short while, and the first thing I noticed placed on a table was a statue of the Raising of the Flag at Iwo Jima.

Next to it was a pair of combat boots symbolizing the many Fallen. The American and Texas flags were positioned beside the boots. A tear rolled down my face. Debi said, "Don't cry. You are about to meet the Governor to honor Joey!"

I wiped my eyes and took a deep breath. The next words I heard were, "The Governor is ready to see you."

We were escorted into the office, and Governor Perry greeted Debi with a handshake and then a hug. I was next and he said, "I am so glad you came!"

While glancing around the office, I noticed photos and paintings of several military heroes. There was a picture of him as an Air Force pilot. Behind his desk was a photo of his father, who was a WWII bomber pilot. On a chair, there was a set of camo fatigues and combat boots.

Propped up against his desk was a painting of the fallen Navy Seal Team 10 from Operation Red Wing and Marcus Luttrell as the Lone Survivor. I have the book and have read it three times. After that, I gave it to Joey, and he took it to Afghanistan. Someday, I would like to meet Marcus and have him sign the book in Joey's honor. The book was among Joey's personal effects that came back from Afghanistan after he died. I also came across a Seal Team 1 coin in those belongings and would love to know who gave it to him and why.

The governor's office was filled with the history of all the heroes he met and honored. It was inspiring to see a leader who loved his country, state, and the people who served in the Armed Forces. The governor continued to point out various items in his office that he cherished. This was an experience I will never forget and will cherish forever.

It was time to open the box containing Joey's Red Lion Colt 45 Auto pistol. I was so proud of it and what it meant to our family. Governor Perry opened the box and picked up the pistol.

I said to him, "You've seen this one before."

We talked about the experience he had at Colt when he first saw the weapon. There was a photographer there taking pictures of this great meeting. Debi brought a photo of Joey with his flight helmet on, posed over his 50-cal. machinegun. Included in the photo was another picture of him in the helicopter, standing there, pointing to his first combat mission near the American Flag. He had a grand smile on his face. The governor, Debi, and I posed with Joey's picture and the pistol. What a memory!

After that, Governor Perry said, "This picture is for me?"

Debi said, "Yes sir," and handed it to him.

He placed it on a side desk, front and center, next to several photos of Heroes that he admired. I was in awe of the moment, seeing Joey's picture being placed there. He truly understands the grief and pain families endure when they lose a loved one to war. I can only begin to thank the governor for his compassion. What a great man!

After we admired the pistol and felt the true meaning of why we were there, he opened a desk drawer and pulled out another box. This was a pistol given to him by Colt, honoring him as Governor of Texas. It had his name engraved on it, the Texas State Seal, Serial #0001, and wooden grips embossed with the Texas Lone Star. It didn't stop there. He asked us, "Do you want to see my carry pistol?"

I said, "Yes!"

He reached under his desk and had me move around so I could see what he was doing. There was a fingerprint-activated scanner that operated a safe that contained the pistol. Naturally, it was another Colt. He unloaded it and checked the chamber. It was chambered in a .357 Sig cartridge. He is a true Texan, pistol and all.

Here is another treat for us. Remember Marcus? A movie will be coming out soon, and Governor Perry had the first look at its trailer. He got out his laptop and played the movie for us. We talked about the Red Lions Project, and I gave him the information. We said our goodbyes and came away with a good feeling about him and Texas.

Approximately a month later, his staff called to inform us that a photo of the event was being sent. After it arrived, there was another surprise included when we opened the box. It was a signed card that read, "Good luck with the Red Lion Project, Governor Rick Perry." I keep that prized photo of the governor, Debi, and me on my desk.

God bless Texas!

LeTourneau University

RECEIVING A PHONE CALL or an email about the Red Lion Project always astounds me. Something is working beyond our control; it comes from a higher source. Faith and belief are what keep me going. This is what led a group of college athletes to honor our Fallen Six.

Early one morning, an email popped up that seemed different. It was from a young lady, Kelsie Benson, a member of the women's softball team for LeTourneau University. She told me the team wanted to honor our Marines for the entire season. And Kelsie wanted us to attend a doubleheader that weekend. Talk about short notice!

Six of the team members would wear special jerseys honoring our men of the Fallen Six. The Lucky Red Lions were going to be playing softball! I could sense the excitement in her words. They would wear them with pride and then give them to us to give to the families.

What's amusing is that a parking ticket Kelsie got on campus started this sequence of events. This ticket turned out to be the turning point and the reason our Lions were chosen. It's strange how things happen, people meet, and amazing events come about.

Kelsie had gone to the Campus Chief of Police to take care of the ticket. She went to his office and noticed all the military photos and plaques on the wall. She inquired whether the Chief had any connections in the military. Chief Terry Turner immediately replied, "Yes, I do. My son is Capt. Mat Turner, USMC."

Kelsie also told the Campus Chief of Police that the University and the women's softball team wanted to honor the fallen and asked if he knew any of our country's fallen heroes. As fate would have it, Terry Turner's son had been assigned to The Lucky Red Lions of 363H in K-Bay, Hawaii. Capt. Mat Turner was also deployed to Afghanistan when the crash that killed our son occurred. Joey was assigned under Turner, a lieutenant at the time, to MAG24 Flight Equipment, a logistics unit that supplies all the flight equipment for helicopter crews.

Capt. Mat Turner knew Joey and the crew personally, as he was a CH53 combat pilot in Afghanistan, along with all the other members of Our Fallen Six. The unit lost six great men that night, and men like Capt. Turner will always remember them.

Well, soon, Kelsie and her teammates made the arrangements. And the day came for us to attend this special honor ceremony in Longview, TX. Kelsie texted us to inquire about our arrival time. And it wasn't long before we were looking at each other on the field. She was so excited, and I was honored.

Her team was warming up for the game, and I enjoyed seeing how intense they were. They were playing UT at Tyler, which was ranked #2 in the country. The opening ceremony began with the announcement of each team member and the fallen hero they represented. Both teams stood at attention for a particular Marine or military soldier.

Chief Terry Turner threw the first pitch, and Kelsie was the catcher. The ladies battled bravely and with all their hearts. Unfortunately, the outcome of the games was not in their favor.

We all gathered after the games were over, and the team signed an official Yellow Jacket ball given to me in honor of our young men. I, in turn, gave them each a pin with the American and Marine flags on it to wear on their hats. I would like to say thank you to LeTourneau University and the ladies of the Yellow Jackets for giving it their all.

The story continues in a way that almost brought me to my knees. Shortly after that, Capt. Matthew Turner had the honor of visiting Iwo Jima and going up to the summit of Mt. Suribachi. Every Marine considers this spot sacred as it commemorates the brave soldiers who died fighting at the top of this mountain.

Have you ever noticed the wrists of our returning Marines and soldiers? A common sight is a bracelet engraved with the name of a friend or fallen hero and the words "Gone but never forgotten." I wear one of these bracelets inscribed with Joey's name.

Shortly after that last deployment, all the former members of HMH363 had bracelets made with each of the names of the Fallen Six. Capt. Turner wore his on the day he went to the top of the summit. It's hard to imagine the thoughts of a Marine in that scenario.

The sacrifices made here symbolized what they stand for: Semper Fi, always loyal, always faithful. Capt. Turner told his father that he wanted to honor all the Marines who fought for their country, especially the Fallen Six. He removed the bracelet and placed it in a special spot at the top of the summit to always remember them.

Six men raised our flag on February 23, 1945, and 68 years later, one man left a bracelet there with six names on it. This is the ultimate honor one Marine can pay to another: *To always remember*.

Who would have thought that the son of a university police chief was a Red Lion who flew CH53s with our crew? And who could have guessed that someone else at the university, initially dealing with just a parking ticket, would end up organizing a celebration for our son at the same place? And that the campus police chief's son, Capt. Mat Turner, was stationed at K-Bay and knew each of the Fallen Six personally.

Without their meeting, this great honor would not have occurred. I call these events "miracles" because they do not happen by chance.

Semper Fi and God bless.

Darkness in Montana

TONIGHT, I decided to go up the mountain and sit in the darkness. The reason is not clear to me. Being alone up here allows all sorts of thoughts to flow through your mind. One question I have is, "Where do I want to be?"

Emotions tell me one thing; the unknowns say another. The future is already laid out for me, but it's hidden from sight. The only light I have is the half moon and all the stars. The skies are so clear up here; no clutter, no big city lights to fade into the deep darkness. I just look up and wonder.

I've been looking back on my life, questioning what I could have or should have done differently. All the good and bad are filtering through the window of darkness. You can see visions of the past, faces that you know, and ones that are gone now. Loneliness surrounds me, and icy darkness fills my soul.

I walk down the dirt road by the glow of the moon guiding my path. The stars seem to spin around, surrounding my thoughts. Looking up at the night sky and the forever of it all makes me feel so small. I think to myself and then say out loud, "How much does one life matter?"

I long for an answer. Sometimes, I sense that I am not alone up here; I know I'm not. There is a presence here that helps me move forward no matter what. I don't feel the cold in the air, only the peace that it brings.

I continue to head uphill toward the highest point on the mountain. Once on top, I just sit on the ground and breathe in the night. I know there are living creatures around me, but they don't matter tonight. There is danger in this country, but everything is silent. All I can hear is the beat of my heart and each breath I take. Being alone with my thoughts brings me into a new reality.

Visions fill my head of a warm, cozy cabin with a glowing fireplace lighting up the room. But still, I am alone. I believe this will be a place of intense reflection and healing. It will be for many who see what I see, feel what I feel, and believe in the miracles of life that are placed before us.

Wandering aimlessly in the dark is a good thing. It breaks the bonds that we sometimes hold too dearly to us. It makes life easier when all you feel is your heartbeat. The fears of the unknown slip away. As I stand to get up and head down the road, I begin to hear sounds. First, it's the crunching of the rocks beneath my feet, the snapping of twigs, and the sound of stiff grass brushing against my pant legs.

My senses have returned to normal, but the mountain remains at rest. I start counting every step I take back to the truck parked at the bottom of the mountain. It's a silly thing to do, but it brings me back to childhood thoughts. I will never be able to retrace these steps.

I open the truck door, get in, and start the engine. Warm air flows from the heater out of the vents. I realize it is in the 30s outside and yearn for that dream of a warm, cozy fireplace to gaze into.

That's what I see in the darkness on the mountain.

Heaven's Gate

EVERYONE WANTS to go to heaven, but this is a story about searching for heaven on earth. The search had brought us to Montana, where we embarked on a several-month-long journey to reach our ultimate destination: Exit 55 on Hwy 90, going west. You see, our search was to find the perfect property for the Red Lion Project site. And sure enough, it appeared like a rainbow after a storm.

The directions to the land were exact. My spirit was lifted when I turned off the paved road onto a dirt mountain trail. Then, we traveled 3.5 miles up a winding road through some of the most beautiful scenery Montana has to offer. Driving through the wilderness gave us the feeling of being the first explorers to set foot on the land. We were excited and eagerly anticipated what was around the next bend.

The sun was slowly setting as evening approached. The forest was changing, with the rays of light streaming between the branches of the trees. A sense of peace that had been missing for a long time came over me. I could see the end of the road, which was blocked by a huge steel pipe gate marking the entrance to the property.

The evening breezes were coming down the mountain, carrying such sweet smells I had never experienced before. The mountain seemed so pristine, clean, and untouched. We got out, opened the gate, and stepped foot on the land for the first time.

While walking around, I felt a sense that told me this was the place. As I looked at my wife, we simultaneously exclaimed, "This is it!"

The next words that were spoken were, "Let's name it 'Heaven's Gate.' This will be Joey's final resting place on his long journey to find peace." And it has been known as that ever since. Each visit to this tranquil and lovely piece of land reminds us that a piece of heaven exists here on earth.

The Birth of a Miracle

Joey had several friends during his short life. Two of his best friends were Lucas ("Luc") and Amanda Frazier. Joey introduced them to each other in high school. They ended up dating, fell in love, and got married.

Luc was so grateful to Joey for playing Cupid and getting them together that they asked me if they could name their firstborn son after him. I was so honored by their asking. They decided to name him Logan Craig Frazier. That would be a name to live up to. But knowing Joey and Luc as they were growing up really made me think, "This baby is going to need a lot of supervision!" Those two were always goofing off and getting into all kinds of shenanigans.

Heaven only knows how many phone calls I received from the principal relaying something that had happened at the school, with me replying, "Joey did WHAT?" But I firmly believe that his laid-back (but rebellious) personality helped him make it in the Marine Corps.

What's interesting is that on January 18, 2013, Amanda Frazier gave birth to a little angel three weeks early, *on the exact date Joey passed away one year before.* God had his mighty hand on this new life—Logan Craig Frazier. This child took away the grief and pain we had gone through that year before. We believe Joey is his guardian angel and will watch over him.

The miracle continued to bear out. One month later, on February 18th, I awoke that morning and looked out the window at the yellow rose bush that had been planted when Joey was born. You may remember me talking about this in a previous story.

A single rose was blooming on Joey's rose bush. I called Debi, and we both marveled at its beauty. I immediately called Luc and Amanda and told them what was happening. They were amazed!

Luc said, "I figured something was going to happen, but nothing like this."

They agreed to come over that day, and we would finally get to meet baby Logan on his one-month birthday. Debi and I held this little man for the first time, and a warm feeling of love flowed through each of us. Debi picked the yellow rose and placed it on Logan's chest—one yellow rose for one little man.

I posted the following on the Red Lions Facebook page to express the significance of the birth of this child:

> We are going to get a visit from Logan Craig Frazier today. He is one month old. To add to the miracle, one yellow rose bloomed on Joey's rose bush! Two yellow roses bloomed on this bush on the one-month date after Joey passed away. The two roses had 22 petals on each of them. He was 22 years old when he left us. We are expecting several more miracles from this little man!

When little Logan was four years old, I received a note from his grandmother, Sherry Martinez, which really got me thinking. She said, "I can tell you personally that your Joey definitely watches over our little Logan. Logan tells us about his talks with him."

I responded, "Thanks for the note. These days are hard on us. This all happened for a reason that we will understand in our own way. Reading about Logan talking to Joey is a miracle! There are special people watching over us."

This was Sherry's reply:

> I can never imagine the pain and heartache that you feel. If you ever want to know what Joey is doing, ask little Logan. He told me that sometimes

they sit on the mountain in the sky and share French fries, chicken nuggets, and chocolate ice cream. This is coming from a 4-year-old! There's no doubt in my mind that miracles from Heaven happen.

Thanks, Little Man.

Blue Balloons

SPECIAL EVENTS happened on the mountain, and this time, my heart and soul were touched by the love you only receive when you hold a new baby.

It was the 28th of August, early in the morning. Andi, our youngest daughter, was expecting her second child any day now! She was still in the Marines, stationed at K-Bay along with her husband, Steven, and first daughter, Aurora.

That day, we had company on the mountain. Dustin, a former Marine assigned to the Pegasus Helicopter Unit, lived in Montana and helped us for a few days with work on the cabins. It's always nice to have a witness when a *gift* comes floating down to greet us first thing in the morning.

Dustin, Debi, and I were out on the porch drinking our morning coffee and discussing what we were going to work on that day. It seems like, on cue, all three of us looked up at a pine tree located right behind the cabin. It must have caught our eye because it was very bright with the morning sun shining on it. At first, we could not make out what it was. All three of us walked up the hill to get a closer look.

Debi said, "It's a balloon."

The morning breeze made it dance around; it glowed with a blue metallic sparkle. The balloon was stuck in the treetop, held in place by thin ribbons. Dustin wanted to climb up and get it, but it was about 40 feet up the tree, and we asked him not to take the chance of falling from that height.

I told him we would work on that later after working on one of the cabins for the day.   We returned to our cabin for lunch and the balloon was gone.

During the time we were down at the lower cabin, Andi called and told us that she had the baby that morning, and they named her Nova Marie.

"Nova!" I said to Debi. "That balloon was in the shape of a blue metallic star."

It came to that mountain top on that little baby's birthday! *Where did it come from,* I thought. The nearest town is over 20 miles away. We returned to the upper cabin and looked up at the treetop, but the balloon wasn't there. I was excited about the new member of our family, but I also felt frustrated that we were not able to retrieve the balloon. I thought I knew who sent it, and, in an instant, it was gone. The experience once again showed me how precious life is and, at the same time, how fragile.

Later that day, we called Andi and told her about the blue balloon. She said, "It was a simple gift welcoming Nova into the world." I searched for the balloon but could not find it.

Not until October, when another Marine came to visit, would my luck change. Retired USMC Gunny Horne was here for a hunting trip. One morning, we decided to hike a game trail behind the upper cabin. We had gone about a mile when something shiny caught my eye.

It was the balloon lying there as if someone had placed it there for us to find it! I told Gunny the story of the balloon and he replied, "Us Marines know how to get our message across."

All I could say was, "Semper Fi."

Sometime later, Andi, Stephen, Aurora, and Nova were back in civilian life and living in their new home in Maryland. I had given the first blue balloon to little Nova on her first birthday, along with a note telling the story of it happening to us in Montana. Someday, she will be old enough to read about it and know who Uncle Joey was.

Well, something incredibly strange happened again! I received a text message from Andi with a picture attached. The message read, "Would you believe it?!"

I opened the picture, and there was Andi standing in her new backyard, holding a blue metallic star-shaped balloon identical to the one that landed on the mountain! Little Nova was standing behind her, wrapped around her mother's leg. I sent her a message right back and said, "You know who sent it." Immediately afterward, I called her to hear how she had found the balloon.

"We were all in the backyard of the new house, just enjoying the day and taking a break from moving in," she began. "I looked over in the corner of the yard and saw something blue under the trees, all crumpled up. I thought it was just some trash that had been blown there by the wind. I went over to pick it up and realized it was another blue metallic Nova balloon, exactly like the one from Montana! I could not believe what I had just found! A few tears ran down my cheek as I showed the balloon to Stephen and the girls."

As I was talking to Andi about what had happened, we both knew who sent the second balloon. It was a housewarming gift, welcoming them to their new home and happy life together. Andi told me that Joey would always be watching over them, especially little Nova. She ended the conversation with the two words all Marines believe in—Semper Fi.

The Cap and the Mug

HAVE YOU EVER realized that random acts of kindness and honor can circle back to you years later, revealing their true significance? This one act hit me hard one evening after Debi and I had attended the Walker County Wounded Warriors Banquet. We had been invited to attend as Gold Star Parents.

Debi, along with four other mothers from our local area, were honored as Gold Star Moms. The ladies were escorted in by Army soldiers as part of the opening ceremony. When Joey's name was called, followed by his mother's, the tears came back like they had so many times before. This marked our second attendance, and we plan to return annually for as long as possible.

The individuals from Walker County who support this event include exceptional military veterans and families. The event is used to raise funds for Brooks Army Medical Center in San Antonio, Texas. This is the place where all our seriously injured military members are taken to receive care. Brooks is an amazing place where great healing takes place: physical, emotional, and spiritual.

After bidding goodnight to everyone who supported our troops, we drove twenty miles south on the freeway. After arriving home, I headed upstairs to my office for some solitude with my thoughts. This room holds all the memories of Joey's three years in the Marines. It is a place of intense feelings and connections that you can only understand once you enter the room.

I refer to my office as "The War Room" because most of the items placed there were in combat with Joey. Sitting near the front window is a table that displays so much of who he was. Looking at the black watch cap with the words "U.S. Marine Corps" and the Eagle, Globe, and Anchor sewn on it brought back to mind one of the first gifts I received from a stranger. Beside the cap was a coffee mug gifted to me by that same man.

This encounter happened in a department store in Dover, Delaware. Debi and I were shopping for a winter coat for her. She did not have a coat warm enough to wear when we had to wait for the remains of our Fallen Six on the tarmac at the airport at Dover Air Force Base. The emotions of anticipation, grief, and confusion were overpowering during that cold January.

Up walks a perfect stranger holding the coffee mug and cap in his hand. I had to ask him where he got them. He mentioned a military shop in the mall that stocked a variety of items like that. I don't know how or why the question came up, but he asked, "What are you doing here?"

"We are waiting for our son to come back from Afghanistan," I replied.

Initially, he smiled. But quickly, he could tell something was wrong. I could not hold it back and sobbed out loud that our son had been killed. All of us stood there and cried. He was an older man and told me he had served in Vietnam in the Marines.

He said, "Here. Take these things. It's the least I can do for you."

I thanked him, and he walked away. I didn't know his name, and even today, I can't recall his face. But the gesture he made will always be with me.

Thank you, kind man. Semper Fi

Two Women, Two Paintings

ART IS A REFLECTION of the soul. Two artists I met use their work to embody the love of God, family, and country—especially our military. These special ladies are Cheryl Kramer Whitfield and Tami Curtis Guy.

I was first contacted by Cheryl shortly after Joey passed. She is the founder of the Fallen Warriors Memorial, which is a monument honoring over 700 fallen heroes from Texas. Cheryl invited Debi and me to a ceremony with other Gold Star families. We gladly accepted the invitation and arrived early to see the memorial. [NOTE: If anyone wants to visit the monument, it is located at 14641 Cutten Road in Houston, TX.]

We walked up to the black granite wall and found Joey's name engraved there. Seeing his name brought back the painful truth of his absence, leaving me emotionally shattered yet again. Tears fell like the downpour of a summer storm.

Debi and I looked around and observed other family members crying and sobbing. (As of today, over 700 names from the Gulf Wars are listed on this memorial.) After we regained our composure, Cheryl told us about an artist, Tami Curtis Guy, from New Orleans. Tami's artwork, displayed at the memorial, was to be given to us after the ceremony.

I must describe all the amazing thoughts that were woven into the painting. One photo, selected from hundreds taken at the memorial, inspired Tami's unbelievable work of art. The striking painting features a soldier standing at the black granite wall and paying tribute to a fallen comrade. Even now, we don't know who the photographer or the soldier was.

If you look at Tami's painting, the soldier is kneeling on one knee with his head bowed. He's dressed in shorts, a T-shirt, a ball cap, and gym shoes. His right hand is pressed against the wall over the name of his fallen friend.

The man wears a memory bracelet on his right wrist. Dog tags dangle from a chain in his left hand.

A reflection of the soldier's hand and arm shines back from the black granite. You can almost see a tear running down the young man's cheek, although a black ball cap shields his face. Beneath his feet are two flags: the American flag and the Texas Lone Star, waving proudly in the breeze. Superimposed on the painting are two soldiers carrying rifles.

The phrase, "Courage is Endurance for One Moment More," is displayed prominently in the painting.

This beautiful work of art is dedicated to the fallen of the Gulf Wars, including:
- Operation New Dawn,
- Operation Enduring Freedom and
- Operation Iraqi Freedom

I have often wondered, *was there any freedom won in these wars?* I'm not sure there was.

The painting's most striking element is an angelic figure. A white, transparent gown adorns the angel. His face is half flesh and half spirit. Finally, his hand rests on the soldier's shoulder as if to console him with an angelic wing stretched over the soldier's back.

All of this is depicted on canvas with paint, and it comes from the heart of Tami Curtis Guy. This masterpiece has hung in my office (aka The War Room) for nearly 13 years. We give Tami our deepest and sincerest thanks.

After the event at the memorial, Cheryl informed us that Tami, whom we'd never met, wished to create a second painting especially for us. Cheryl reported Tami had seen a picture of Joey in an article she'd read. From over 600 fallen soldiers, she desired to paint a memorial portrait of one—our son. I willingly provided information so Tami could contact us about the painting.

Well, sure enough, Tami called us later that week and said that after reading the article about Joey and viewing his photo, she *had* to paint something in his honor! Once again, the emotions began to overwhelm me.

When we initially visited, she asked, "What do you want in the painting?"

I replied, "A lion" to represent his unit and the Fallen Six. After that, the rest was up to her. Tami told us she preferred an in-person meeting before starting the painting.

After a few phone calls, we arranged to meet Tami in New Orleans one week before Super Bowl 2013, featuring the Baltimore Ravens and the San Francisco Giants. From our home to New Orleans, it is over 350 miles. But Debi and I quickly planned the trip and were fortunate to find a hotel room there during Super Bowl week on such short notice! (By the way, the score ended up 34-31 with a Ravens win!)

That first year had gone by in such a blur; grief and disbelief caused the days and nights to pass by in a blur. So, meeting Tami for the first time helped change my life for the better. Just viewing one of her paintings renewed my faith in God. The question of "Why?" began to soften. There are good people who are placed into your life for a reason. Tami's spiritual vision, translated onto the canvas, really touched my heart.

She created the beautiful painting below. As I describe the Red Lion painting, you will hopefully understand these memories.

Tami Curtis Guy, who lives in Mississippi, is the Commissioned Artist who painted these for the memorial of the Fallen Heroes. This one was painted for Joey's family.

The main theme and focal point are a massive male lion lying with a lamb nestled against the lion. Below the beast and his prey, written on a background of green grass, is the Bible verse Proverbs 28:1, which reads: *The righteous are as bold as a lion.*

On the bottom corners of the painting are two beautiful yellow roses, a reminder of Joey's miracle rose bush that dropped 22 petals. The lion is truly amazing because his flowing mane has tints of red. His most striking feature is his piercing, sky-blue eyes. Tami created the painting from a photo of Joey taken in Afghanistan. Joey's bright blue eyes twinkled with an expression that said, "Look what I'm doing!"

The eagle, globe, and anchor (EGA) in the upper left corner of the painting symbolize the United States Marine Corps' past, present, and future. The lucky red lion, which has been the emblem of the 363 Unit since 1952, is in the upper right corner.

Behind the lion stands Joey's cross, which is 4' tall and 3' wide. Carved in the center of the cross is the Red Lion, which is painted on all the unit's helicopters. At the base of the cross is an American flag. In the background is the endless forest and a glimpse of the Rocky Mountains. The last feature in Tami's painting is a stunning rainbow coming down to the earth at the base of Joey's cross.

Before closing out this chapter, I want to describe our visit to Audubon Park in New Orleans. While there, Tami asked Debi and I if we would like to view a statue at the park. She said it embodied the theme of the Red Lion project in Montana (and the reason for this book!).

As we walked through the park, I felt that something amazing was going to happen. The three of us walked along paths that bordered a long, winding bayou. Along the bank stood ancient live oak trees garnished with Spanish moss. It was like taking a step back in time.

Around the next bend of the trail stood the statue: a life-size bronze carving of a father and son going fishing! They both carried cane poles and were headed to the bayou. Both figures had smiles on their faces, just as Joey and I had displayed while we were on our trip.

The reality of it all hit me as I remembered our 16,000-mile trip. If only we could have taken one more fishing trip together! Tami, Debi, and I stood quietly there viewing that statue, which had weathered into a worn, gray-green color. We walked around it from all sides and took in the reality of what it represented. Of course, I snagged several photos, as well. Following a final goodbye and thanks to Tami, we headed back to our motel.

Several months later, another beautiful painting, created in honor of our Joey by Tami Curtis Guy, was delivered to our home. It is the Lion and the Lamb described earlier. It proudly hangs in the War Room along with the Red Lions painting.

A Special Email

SOMETIMES, there are things in life that are just meant to be. With all the contacts from people connected with our Fallen Six, it is not unusual to have an e-mail pop up on the Red Lions website that really astounds me. This is one that brought the meaning of the Brotherhood of the Marine Corps, Semper Fi. It started out with an introduction:

> My name is Nathan Navarro, formerly known as CPL Navarro USMC 2nd Battalion 4th Marines Fox Company 2nd Platoon. I was deployed to Musa Qala, Helmand Province, from 2011 to 2012. The Fallen Six died in an attempt to resupply my platoon when we ran out of food and water. For years, we have tried to locate the names of the Marines who died for us. Luckily, after joining an Irreverent Warriors Hike in Denver, I was able to talk to another former Marine who had known the Fallen Six and was able to link me up to the website. I would just like to speak on behalf of my platoon that your son, as well as the rest of his squadron, can now be honored properly. I have already sent out their names to everyone I can reach from my platoon. We are all at ease now being able to put a name to the warriors who sacrificed everything to help their brothers. THANK YOU, SEMPER FI.

Nathan continued to send a few text messages and phone calls while we were in Montana, and we agreed to meet someday. I was looking forward to it. However, a forest fire hit Montana, and the hurricane hit Houston, so life got crazy for both of us.

Debi and I had just returned from Montana in late October when I received another text from Nathan. He said that two of the Marines who were out there that night Joey died were coming to visit him in November. He lives in Spring, Texas, just a short twenty-minute drive from our home in Willis, and so we were excited to visit Nathan and his fellow Marines.

The day finally came when we would meet in person on November 19th. Nathan called to say, "We are on our way. Where do you want to meet for dinner?"

We agreed to meet on the front steps of a local restaurant in Conroe, the city neighboring our hometown. Debi and I arrived and parked the car. You can easily identify a Marine when you see one. Three great heroes, tall and strong, were standing there on the steps.

I walked up to them and said, "You all must be the Marines!"

They looked at us with a proud smile and said, "Yes, sir. I'm glad to meet you."

We all shook hands and exchanged names: Nathan Navarro, Edwin Lopez, and Hayden Garrett. We were all hungry for a good meal, so we happily went inside to catch up. Nathan told me that when they were out at the F.O.B., the unit was down to the last few bottles of water and only two MRE meals per man. That was the reason our Red Lions had flown out that night!

I explained to him that a Marine in Joey's unit told me Joey wasn't required to fly that night, but he knew the troops desperately needed supplies. The bond those men have for each other is so strong that they will do anything for each other. Hearing this made them feel so much better and at ease with what happened.

Nathan said that they could not have supplies delivered any other way because of the many IEDs on the roads leading to them. It must have been helpless to be left out there. Nathan and Hayden were mine sweepers, going out day in and day out, risking their lives.

During the meal, they wanted to hear about the Red Lions Project and the fishing in Montana. Nathan said he was going to buy a kayak to bring up there to fish the Clark Fork River. These three men loved the outdoors and would fit in just fine up on the mountain. I couldn't stop telling them how much it meant to us to meet them.

A special guest joined us for dinner that evening, Jim Reinhard, father of CPL. Kevin Reinhard. Jim and I have become good friends since our sons went down in the crash. We formed a bond, much like our Marines, which cannot be broken.

Jim called me earlier in the week and said he had some time off from work and wanted to come out and visit for a few days. He lives and works in Baton Rouge, Louisiana, about a five-hour drive from our home in Texas. What a surprise for him to learn that the Marines were coming to visit. He said several times, "How is all this continuing to happen?" We both know our boys are watching over us from heaven.

We were about to finish dinner, and I asked the men if they wanted to come out to the house for a few Red Lion beers. Debi gave Nathan our home address, which he then entered into his smartphone's GPS. We left the parking lot before them, yet they beat us to the house and were parked outside when we arrived. Talk about being ready for a beer!

All of us went up to my office, the War Room, where all the military achievements from our family were displayed. The history contained in this room starts with my grandfather Joseph Cioci's discharge papers from WWI. It then displays my dad's photo from WWII and ends with memorabilia from an uncle who was a corpsman in Korea to my Vietnam era. Also proudly displayed are all the accomplishments and commendations by Joey, Tommy, and Andi, who have served now. My goal is to put together a thorough list of all family members with a history of service.

That evening, I passed around a Red Lion Beer to each of the men, and we toasted our Fallen Six heroes. Our conversation centered less on the war and more on their current lives and future prospects. Their presence alone, just these three Marines, spoke volumes about their character.

Time had passed so quickly, and before you knew it, it was 11:00 p.m. We said our goodbyes and promised to "see you on the mountain." It would be great for them to see Joey's dream come true. They gave me a parting gift of a T-shirt of their unit signed by them and told me that the other members would come to Red Lion Mountain to sign it.

Semper Fi, Marines.

The Fallen Six Memorial from Afghanistan

ON DECEMBER 30, 2014, I received a phone call from Kathleen Reinhard, the mother of CPL. Kevin Reinhard. She and her husband, Jim, had received a surprise visit from Staff Sgt. Christopher West. Sargeant West served with the 363 during the deployment when our crew went down.

Sgt. West had brought the Reinhards an unusual gift. It was a plague made from two 4'x4' sheets of plywood. On it was painted, "Gone but not forgotten" and the names of our crew. Along with that gift to the Reinhards, an amazing story was about to unfold!

Chris West told them that he had just returned from Afghanistan, where he had been deployed again. During this deployment, they would be closing down Camp Leatherneck and bringing back the troops. 14 years of fighting in this country, and now it was over, although the loss of lives and the scars from those who came back will always be there.

Breaking down a military base in a combat zone is a huge undertaking. Some things return, but much is lost. If not for Sgt. West, this piece of Red Lion history would have been thrown on the burn pile and gone up in smoke.

The plaque had been taken down after the 363 left the country and went back to K-Bay in Hawaii. It never made the trip. Stored somewhere on Camp Leatherneck, it stayed hidden for almost three years. That in itself is amazing!

Thousands of Marines, Army, and NATO troops were deployed there during that time. Time has its way of making things and memories fade away. This almost happened to this sign honoring our crew.

The Marines assigned to clean up the base were taking down everything, and this plaque was thrown on the burn pile of scrap lumber. However, Sgt. West saw the sign and quickly jumped into action. He explained to the Marines who these legendary figures were, saving the sign from being destroyed by fire.

What are the odds of him being there to see what was going to happen? What are the chances of this piece of plywood being used for some other purpose long before he saw it? There is a guiding hand moving through our lives, and I call this simply a miracle.

After retrieving the sign, now Sgt. West had to figure out what to do with it and how to get it back to the States. As is typical, a Marine's ability to solve a problem kicked in. The helicopters assigned there were coming back with the unit. Here was its ticket home!

With the help of others, they concealed it in one of the helicopters, and it was on its way home. Sgt. West is a great Marine and friend to do such a wonderful thing to preserve this piece of history. Then, on top of that, bring it all the way to the Reinhards.

I was in awe after Kathleen explained what he had done. She told Sgt. West, "I know right where this is going, the Red Lions Project in Montana."

It is humbling and an honor to have such a prominent memorial to our Heroes on display for all who visit.

Thank you, Staff Sgt. Christopher Lee West, USMC.

Semper Fi and God Bess.

The H.E.A.R.T.S. Museum

THE H.E.A.R.T.S. MUSEUM in Huntsville, TX, has become a very important part of my life. The acronym stands for **H**elping **E**very **A**merican **R**emember **T**hrough **S**erving. I walked through their doors shortly after Joey died in Afghanistan, holding the fatigues he wore in combat in my hand. I wanted to donate them to the museum. There was a reason I was drawn to this place, and now I know why.

Walking up to the front desk, I asked if I could donate Joey's clothes for display. The next thing I knew, I found myself seated in a chair with a group of veterans around me. I had broken down crying, and these men didn't even have to ask why. They had *all* faced what I was going through.

An old WWII veteran approached me and asked if I would like to walk around the displays and talk. His presence was calming, so I joined him. As we passed by all the history on the walls, it seemed to come alive.

The museum's history features numerous stories of brave soldiers who served their country, from the Revolutionary War to the current War on Terror, where Joey lost his life. The entire museum is filled with Texas Heroes. What better place to remember Joey in the presence of so many great men and women? The museum took his uniforms, and they will be proudly displayed, honoring a Patriot who loved his country.

All the folks who work there are volunteers who have served their country. I am becoming part of this family by volunteering there myself, doing my part to honor the fallen. I met two ladies who are part of a group that makes quilts for our troops. They meet once a week and sew beautiful patches of material into works of love for our military.

One day, as I sat at the front desk, a loving lady named Maria Martinez approached me and gave me a quilted lap blanket that the ladies had made.

"This is for your son, Joey," Maria shared.

I took it, and the tears started again. It was made entirely from various patterns of red, white, and blue material, featuring photos of Marines in dress blues, along with jets, tanks, and stars. Just this week, I spoke to Carol Olson, who sews the quilts. She told me that she was the one who made Joey's quilt. I thanked her, and a tear came to her eye. She told me she had gotten the material at Brooks Army Medical Center in San Antonio when she was visiting the severely injured troops in the hospital there.

Each year around Christmas, OME (Operation Military Embrace), a wonderful support organization, gives the troops a free BX (Base Exchange). This is basically where they offer consumer goods and services that have been collected through donations year-round. These gifts assist the troops and their families in getting through the hard and healing times.

A designated bolt of cloth was given to Carol, who used it to create quilts for the troops. It came full circle! This time, I received it, and what comfort it is when I think of Joey. Needless to say, it will be treasured—always.

Thank you, H.E.A.R.T.S.

Home of the Brave Quilt

SPEAKING OF QUILTS, another amazing story happened following Joey's death. So many people expressed their gratitude for our son's sacrifice for this country. This is one of the most heartwarming stories we've encountered.

A dear lady named Judy Aswad from a group called the Tomball Quilting Ladies contacted us on February 11, 2013. The call came as a complete surprise. Judy had heard about Joey from a TV news report and told us that her group wanted to make a quilt in his honor.

I didn't know what to say! She mentioned that they had been creating quilts for families of The Fallen and sending them across the country. Judy said it would be an honor to make a quilt for "one of our own, a true Texan, who fought for freedom."

She asked what kind of material we wanted and what size. I turned the phone over to Debi, and she exclaimed, "King size, of course!"

We were unsure about the material to use. But Debi came to me the next day and said, "We could use his fatigue uniforms and flight suits." I told her it was a great idea. We had received all his uniforms from the Marine Corps, and they were just sitting in boxes, never to be worn or used again.

However, sorting through those boxes to select his clothes was one of the most difficult tasks I've ever completed. Just knowing he wore them in combat, fighting, flying, and ultimately dying in these clothes was almost more than I could take. You could *smell* the war on them.

We met up with Judy and gave her Joey's clothing. Naturally, it was an emotional meeting. A year later, Debi and I acquired a stunning quilt from the Tomball Quilting Ladies. It was an amazing work of art, and as you look at it, the love and heartache it represented were stunning. Intricate pieces of fabric, representing the many battles and challenges our son had faced during a time of war, were now intricately woven into a beautiful work of art. Judy told me that the ladies cried when they made the first cut into the fabric. They knew this was part of him.

The quilt embodies Joey's spirit and will remain a treasured memento in our family. It symbolizes the bravery of a young man, almost as if the quilt is trying to communicate its importance to viewers.

Debi and I brought the quilt home and placed it on Joey's bed in the upstairs bedroom. There, it will rest as he did. Looking at it instantly brings tears to my eyes. Just imagining him wearing those same clothes while fighting in a war is so very hard to deal with. His blood, sweat, and life are part of the patchwork that makes up the quilt. I sometimes wonder, *if each piece of cloth could tell its story, what would it say?* The experiences of a young Marine in war are only truly known by the one in uniform.

Often, I sleep in his room, but one night, I decided to sleep under the quilt. I had never done so before, but as soon as I pulled it over me, I felt strangely at peace. It felt as if Joey approved of the quilt and was very proud of it.

The house was empty that night; Debi was babysitting our daughter Tricia's three children. Since Joey's passing, I rarely sleep through the night and encounter dreams that startle me awake. However, that night was one I will never forget.

At some point, I woke up with a jolt. What woke me was a loud and clear voice. There was no mistaking whose voice it was. He said, "Hey, Dad."

I sat up smiling and then tears ran down my face. Joey briefly appeared to approve of the quilt and to offer me comfort, just like the quilt did. He was telling me he was all right.

FISHING WITH JOEY

This is our "Thank You" to the participants in the Home of the Brave Quilt Project:

I am Tom Logan, and my wife, Debi, would like to thank you so very much for sending the quilt honoring Joey, our son. When Debi received the phone call from you a few weeks ago, she told me that someone wanted to send us a quilt for our Fallen Hero. She didn't get any information and was only asked for our mailing address.

We did not know what to expect or from whom it was coming. Since Joey died, we have received so many cards and gifts, and it is so hard to read and look at them. It seems like at any time he will come walking through the door with that great big grin on his face.

Today, the package came in the mail, and Debi said, "This must be the quilt!" She told me to hurry up and open it. What a wonderful surprise as we unfolded it and laid it on our bed. It was beautiful, a labor of love and respect for our young Marine. We taught our son first to love God, then his family, and his country.

He was so very proud to serve. When I read the patch on the corner of the quilt and saw Joey's name handwritten and the message below, tears ran down my face. They were tears of happiness because this quilt comes from people we did not know, who love our country as much as we do. We will cherish it dearly and place it for all to see in our home.

After admiring the quilt and the Uncle Sam bears, I read the history of the Sanitary Commission Quilts. What a lesson in history to be carried on to this day. I only wish that war did not exist and that our young men and women would all come home.

I often wonder what Joey would have become if he had made it back. He lived life to the fullest, never looking back. He loved to fly and fight—what more could a man ask for? He always had a smile on his face, even in the darkest moments.

I noticed that you did not leave any contact information except the return address on the box. Your organization needs to be thanked for what you all are doing. This quilt certainly brightened our day. Lately, Joey has been on my mind a lot, and then a lovely gift arrived at the door out of nowhere. I believe that we still have a great country and will make it through the hard times we are in, thanks to people like you.

Kind Words from the Commander

A FEW WEEKS BACK, I was invited by the family of one of our Fallen Heroes to officiate at his Memorial service. Joseph Logan was one of six Marines who died in a Helo crash on January 19, 2012. It was uncommon for an Air Force Mortuary Affairs Operation chaplain to be part of the returning process for our fallen soldiers. In this situation, the family had made a sincere request, and it was difficult not to honor that request, remembering that families came first.

I arrived in Houston on Sunday evening, knowing that Cpl. Logan was due to arrive Monday morning at Bush Intercontinental Airport, less than two miles away. At about 8:30 a.m., I left the hotel and punched the address into my GPS. As I prepared to turn out of the parking lot on that beautiful cloudless blue-sky morning, I realized I did not need the GPS!

Passing in front of me at that very moment were about 30 members of the Patriot Guard Riders. I had no doubt where they were going, nor why. I fell behind the last of them and let them lead me to the terminal where Cpl. Logan would be arriving.

By 9:00 a.m. I was arriving at the private terminal at the west end of the airfield, where Joseph was due to arrive at 10:00 a.m. As I parked my rental and headed toward the small terminal, I was taken by the number of Patriot Guard members who were already there. Their chaplain said a prayer for Cpl. Logan and a safe procession home.

I passed by a group dressed in leather jackets with patches representing their military background, state, and other symbols like eagles, flags, and

Harley wings. I passed by, greeting many and thanked them for the service they provided to so many families throughout Texas. Some were clean-shaven; others wore beards of various shades of gray and hair pulled back into ponytails. But they all had one common goal that morning: to honor one of our Fallen.

Soon, I was among more than 50 police officers in their fresh-pressed uniforms. They, too, had gathered to not only serve as escorts but to honor a fallen service member. Moments later, I found the Casualty Assistance Calls Officer (CACO, who serves as a liaison of the family) and Cpl. Logan's family. We greeted each other, shared a few words, and hugged one another.

While waiting for the Marine Honor Guard to get things in order for the flight line and for the Kalitta jet to arrive, Cpl. Logan's family shared touching stories about him. His dad took time to express his gratitude for all the support they had received while in Dover for Joseph's Dignified Transfer. I noted how touched they were as well by the support from the Friends of the Fallen and the USO.

Soon, it was time for the family to make their way outside and welcome their son, Joseph, home. This was not what they had expected or the homecoming they had looked forward to, but sometimes life is that way. Joseph's mom, dad, and wife took seats with the Marine escort at their side. Just ahead to their left were more than 100 Patriot Guard members, each standing in formation holding a 3.5 x 5-foot American flag. Ahead of them were several dozen police officers, also in their formation. To their right were the hearse and the Marine Honor Guard.

A few cameras could be heard clicking as we all took in the special moment together. Perhaps five minutes later, a white SUV with flashing lights made its way onto the airfield. It would act as the escort for the Kalitta jet taxiing into position from the east end of the runway. As it moved closer, it was obvious that air traffic overhead had been placed in a holding pattern as news outlet helicopters moved in to record the unfolding event below.

As the jet finished getting into position and shut down the engines, the Patriot Guard members circled the aircraft and were called to attention. Even though their ages varied greatly, and few looked like what they did when they wore the uniform of their respective service, they each snapped to reverent attention. The American flag was proudly displayed in front of each of them. Seconds later, an officer called the police to attention as well. Then, all the Marines and other service members present were called to attention.

Out of the corner of my eye, I could see tears streaming down the faces of the family members as the flag-draped casket was moved into full view from the rear of the aircraft. The honor guard on command marched respectfully and with precision into place alongside the casket. Within seconds, Cpl. Joseph D. Logan's casket passed in front of us and was placed inside the hearse.

With one call, all who had gathered were dismissed and made their way to their cars for the procession to Joseph's hometown of Willis, some 58 miles up the interstate. Amidst the hugs and tears of family and friends, the Patriot Guard and police made their way from the airfield to the cars and motorcycles. There was an overwhelming sense of respect for one who had died far too early in life—for this young man who stepped up and signed on the line to serve his country in the midst of an ongoing war.

Within minutes, all had made their way to their vehicles. The motorcycles of the guard members and police roared to life, and the procession began to snake its way from the terminal to the interstate. I was told afterward there were over 400 motorcycles involved! I immediately noticed that, as we passed each intersection, all traffic had come to a halt; people had exited their cars and were solemnly standing by. A short time later, we curled up the ramp onto the interstate, led by both the Patriot Guard and the police—but there was no traffic! There were no cars to be seen anywhere up ahead.

It took me a few moments to comprehend what I was not only witnessing, but engaged in. To rightly honor this valiant young man, all northbound traffic had been stopped. And not just in one lane, but in all six lanes! For the next 58 miles, I witnessed one of the most heart-wrenching and compelling events of my life. It was a two to three-mile procession led by a group of ragtag, flag-bearing, motorcycle-riding patriots and uniformed officers, followed by family and friends, and more police scattered throughout. And to reiterate, there was no traffic!

Along the way, we passed on-ramps, where occupants had gathered at the edge of the road to share this young Marine's journey home. On the other side of the interstate, cars and trucks of all types pulled toward the jersey wall, and they stood silently by. I couldn't help but notice that there were people of all ages and skin color, men, women, and children, too. I was moved to tears time and time again as we traveled toward Joseph's hometown.

We passed a mom, perhaps 30 years old, and her son, who looked to be around seven years old. He was sitting on the jersey wall holding a small American flag, with Mom standing behind him. Neither of them moved as we passed by. *What did she say to him?* I wondered. How had she explained this to her young son?

A few miles down the road, an overpass crossed the highway. Hanging from it was a large American flag, and from one end to the other, the overpass was lined with citizens displaying flags. The tears began again. I could only imagine what his family was thinking when we passed an outlet mall that had dedicated their huge digital sign to Cpl. Logan. There, in view of everyone who passed that way, was a full-size picture of Joseph in his dress blues. The caption read, "In Honor of CLP. Joseph Logan."

Time and time again, as oncoming traffic realized what this procession was, they stopped and paid homage and, in their own way, thanked a fallen service member for his service. If there was any doubt about the patriotism of the citizens of this country, it was dispelled as we traveled those 58 miles.

Once we reached his hometown, our procession continued down Main Street. It was filled with people, some having left their place of business, others having made their way here for this very moment. We turned right and then left, and the procession and Joseph passed in front of his home one last time. Even here, the streets were lined with people, some holding signs celebrating his life, others with small signs that said, "Rest in peace."

At last, we pulled into the funeral home. Here, Joseph's family members were able, for the first time since his return to U.S. soil, to lay their hands on the flag draping the casket of their loved one. This was their time. We all stepped aside and gave them the privacy that they deserved. As they shed their tears, one could also see the relief on their faces. Their Joseph was home! And all along the way, hundreds if not thousands of people had stopped to say thank you to Joseph and his family for his sacrifice and service!

Lt. Commander Charles Rowley

Extended Memories

Medals & Awards
Cpl. Joseph Daniel Logan USMC

- Hawaii Medal of Honor
- Purple Heart
- Air Medal w/Bronze "1" (Strike/Flight Award)
- Navy Unit Commendation
- Meritorious Unit Commendation (Navy)
- Marine Corps Good Conduct Medal
- National Defense Service Medal
- Afghanistan Campaign Medal W/2 Bronze Campaign Stars
- Global War on Terrorism Service Medal
- Sea Service Deployment Ribbon W/1 Bronze Star
- NATO Medal ISAF Afghanistan
- Rifle Sharpshooter Badge
- Pistol Expert Badge
- Entitled to a blood stripe for NCO Rank
- Air Medal (*second award*) HMH 363
- Combat Air Wings w/3 Star Cluster
- Aerial Observer Award –CH-53 Sea Stallion
- State of Texas House Resolution No.190- 83rd Legislature
- V.F.W. Memorial Commendation Post #4709
- Navy and Marine Corps Achievement Medal
- Air Crew Survival Award

THOMAS LOGAN

Mr. Logan,

To be honest, I've been putting off writing this for far too long, but I think on this significant yet difficult day, it's high time I finally man up and do it.

I served with Joe in HMH-363 and went to Afghanistan with him. That being said, I can't stand Marines. I believe them to be crude, brash, and generally unpleasant. I usually kept to myself, maintained my distance when I could, and just did my job.

But Joe was different. There were some bad days in Afghanistan. The hours were long, the work hard, and the environment was miserable. But Joe never failed to waltz into our shop [usually when he heard we had food] with a goofy smile on his face, a can't-keep-me-down demeanor, and a lame joke to tell.

I cannot express in words how easy your son made it to forget for a moment that we were in a hostile country to fight a war. The last day I saw him, he came by and asked me if he could borrow my Star Wars DVDs. I told him that we had some downtime and were just about to sit down and watch it, but he had a flight soon, so we postponed it till he got back to watch in the flight shop [they had a big screen TV].

After the news came later that night about Iron Tail 06, I didn't cry. I knew I should have. That was one of the few actual friends I had in the Marine Corps, and he was gone. But I never cried.

It was almost surreal to see those around me shedding tears, knowing that I should be among them, but it didn't sink in until a couple of days later when Mark Stoltenberg came into our shop and tossed down my Star Wars DVDs on the table. It hit me instantly, and I lost it. My friend was gone, and suddenly I began to question if I had been the kind of friend to him that he had been to me. What if there had been more I could have done to brighten his day the way he had brightened ours?

I have to admit that when I first heard about the Red Lion Project, I had to chuckle because even though he was gone, his spirit lives on in that project, improving the lives of his brothers and sisters in arms. Just know that today, his memory lives on, and I'll do everything I can to make sure that never changes.

I cannot thank you and your family enough for raising such an amazing man, and I want to let you know that he is constantly in my thoughts and prayers, and in those of the lives he has touched.

Semper Fidelis and God Bless, Cpl. Adam Austin

I opened my e-mails at 9:97 am on the 20th of January 2018 and checked the Red Lion site first to see if anything came in overnight. To my surprise, there was an e-mail from Captain Pete Stachowski. He was one of the pilots from the unit in Afghanistan on the last deployment, the Sundown Mission. What I read next was a touching message that really hit me with the true meaning of a Marine:

> 2:29 am - Tom, I was on the first of two flights that night. I high-fived everyone aboard as I swapped out, and Nate McHone climbed aboard between the first and second missions. 45 minutes later, I got the worst news of my life. I've been procrastinating, but I need to make it out there. I don't know what else to say. I'm sorry I haven't communicated sooner. I'd like to see you soon and shake your hand. Joey was one of the happiest people I've ever met. He and they are ABSOLUTELY not forgotten.

After reading this, it was apparent Pete should have been on that flight, but for whatever reason, he was spared and came home. I could tell that this was very heavy on his heart and mind. The date and time, January 20th at 2:29 am, would have been the morning after the crash, only six years later. That's a lot to live with all those years, and so I responded with the following message:

> Pete, thank you for sharing this with me. It means a lot to us when you all contact us and remember our great Marines. Joey had a big heart and a kind soul. He loved what he was doing and would not have had it any other way. The kid had a smile on his face no matter what. One of the men in the unit told me you were either laughing with him or at him; that's the kind of man he was. He loved the Marines and you all so much that his last phone call home that morning was amazing. He wanted to buy some land in Montana and build a cabin so his Marines could come up and visit. He went on to say that he wanted to live up there, get a job, go in the outdoors, find a good woman, raise a family, and live a simple life. He was telling me about my lifelong dream that he and I talked about when we

hunted and fished together. What an amazing young man to think of this! By his passing, he handed me the greatest gift I have ever been given. We are working on the mountain so we can share his dream with you all. Feel free to contact us anytime. Live your life to the max and make a difference in this world. I hope to see you on the mountain someday to enjoy what he loved. Semper Fi and God bless.

I am also including this letter from Mark Stoltenberg, another great Marine who served with Joey. This young man sent me an email (below) telling us how much Joey meant to them as a brother. Mark came to visit us in Willis and gave me his first Red Lion pistol as a gift and a remembrance for Joey. He told me he had purchased two of them, one for his father and one for himself. He wanted me to have his pistol as a remembrance of Joey and their friendship. This was a once-in-a-lifetime gift that I will always cherish. Semper Fi, Mark.

> Mr. Logan,
> Yes, we live really close. Joe and I claimed Houston and our other bubby in the shop, who is from Fort Worth. Yes, mine and Joe's last boss from the last deployment had been in contact with me after the accident. He was Capt. Will Recalde, I believe you met him in Dover when Joe arrived in the U.S.
> Well, he passed the word that you mentioned if we had any pictures of Joe, you would like them. The only way I could think of to get them to you was by my parents. Since I know they planned on attending Joe's ceremony, they could try to get them to you and Mrs. Logan. I am glad you enjoyed them, (we spoke afterwards about the photos). You know I've been in Joe's immediate shop since he got to go out with the squadron's last deployment in Afghanistan. Joe and I have been night crew together out here for the last 3 months. We had quite a time on the night crew together! I know you have heard a lot of stuff from a lot of people, but I have to tell you, Joe TRULY loved to fly. He would come to work mad if he wasn't on the flight schedule.

FISHING WITH JOEY

Working out and flying is what Joe cared about during this deployment. God, that boy seriously loved to fly! Did Joe tell you that when he earned his Aircrew Combat Wings, the base 2 Star General pinned them on him? He was so proud of the damned coin the general gave him. [*I have the Air Wings, Medal, and Coin; it all came back with his property from Afghanistan.*]

What a HA [Hard Ass] he was ...You know your son was one hell of a hard worker, too! Seriously, I'm his direct boss/ co-worker. Joe was seriously a GET IT DONE, NO EXCUSES guy. I could trust Joe in any aspect of our job, and I mean that.

I don't know if you know, but he was such a hard worker and AO (aerial observer) that out of ALL new AOs in the squadron(about 15), Joe was 2 of 15 that was authorized to man a crew position with a gun,(50 cal.) unsupivised. He showed that much discipline and knowledge when it came to his job. I kid you not; it's rough out here now without Joe...It's total quietness in the shop when I used to have my friend here to talk with and work with, but he's in a better place.

Joe talked of you quite often. Always talking about hunting and how he wanted to take you to Canada on a hunting trip. He said he owed you one for putting up with him. He couldn't make up his mind if he wanted to take you to Canada, fly you to Hawaii, or buy you a pistol, but needless to say, he definitely talked about you often. [*After Joey's passing, I received many of these gifts: two Red Lion pistols, a trip to Hawaii, and all of the hunting and fishing in Montana. The only person missing was him.*]

I and some of the boys (his immediate shop) are for sure coming to meet y'all and share stories about Joe if that's something you wouldn't mind. I and Evan, another guy in my shop, get out of the Marines on May 15th and would like to come around then if y'all will be around.

Well, I hope the email isn't too impersonal; I would love to tell you every story I have of Joe in person. I'm just stuck in this shitty place (Afghanistan), waiting to go home. You know I hope the photos did help you see how really happy Joe was in what he was doing. It wasn't fake, or it wasn't (BS) to make y'all think he was happy; HE WAS, I mean it!

The night of the wreck, I harassed him and all the "fly boys" about how they better bring back a cooler of good stuff. Joe was the first person to tell me to stop being lazy and go get my own food with a smile. lol. Me and Joe used to have an "eating contest" on who could eat the most, so it was a joke amongst us always about food.

Mr. Logan, please know that your son was a very honorable, dependable guy, and we all considered Joe our brother. I don't mean that in a Marine Corps comradery way. I mean that sincerely, Joe was our boy and our friend and co-worker. I'll never forget him and can't wait to meet y'all and see the home Joe grew up in if y'all would have us up. Please feel free to email me if you have anything, anything at all, you would like to ask or know about Joe.

Here's another email from Ricky about Joey:

I just wanted to take a couple of minutes to tell you and your family that I am truly sorry for what has happened. We worked closely with Joe in the shop, and he was an awesome Marine. But what's even more important is that he was an awesome person and friend. We miss him dearly in the shop every day, and we constantly tell his stories back and forth.

Joe made us laugh regularly, whether with him or at him. He was quite a character, lol. I remember the first day I met him on my birthday in Hawaii. Joe was only 20 and wanted a shot of Jägermeister. Now, Joe was still working at MALS, and I had no idea who this kid was.

But I tell you what: I have never seen someone so happy as when we brought him back one! Ha Ha Ha. Joe always enjoyed the little things like that, and he fit right in when he joined our shop. We used to tease him about using rope for dental floss, and he took it in stride and hit us with some good ones right back as he giggled himself to tears. He was always in good spirits.

I really hope that we get to meet sometime. I am from Tyler, TX, but I will be moving to the Ft. Worth area when I get out in October, so it should work out easily enough. Your son was a brother to us, and we would do anything for him, just as he would for us. Y'all are in our prayers. Please let me know if I can do anything at all for y'all. Sincerely, Ricky

FISHING WITH JOEY

It amazes me how so many people, places, and things come together. The memories of war and the men who fought them are always there. This is the case of one young Marine, James Boswell. He was a member of the HMH 363 RED LIONS on the deployment when Iron Tail 06 went down.

James contacted me, along with his mother, Candace Lea, about a picture he took of a helicopter. At first, it was a photo of a beautiful sunset and a helicopter sitting on the tarmac. The deployment was the Red Lions' sundown mission, and after returning from Afghanistan, the unit was going to be disbanded. The unit had been in existence for 60 years as a combat support air wing. The event that was to take place would make this photo a memorial for our Fallen Six.

This helicopter was #45, the one they flew the very next night in the crash. No one could have known. James sent this photo back to his mother, and she made a memorial sign honoring our men. They both wanted to know if I wanted a copy of this part of our son's life in the Marines. The answer was yes! It would mean a lot to us, and we would cherish it.

About a week later, I received the picture, and the emotions welled up again. This sign will be placed in the Cabins in Montana as a memorial to honor and remember our crew of great Marines.

> Thank you again, James and Candace.
> Semper Fi, and God bless all our troops.

The following message tells what makes a Marine. James sent this to me along with a photo of the bird:

> Hello Mr. Logan,
> I deployed with your son and flew alongside him. A while back, my mom had some signs made, and she was unable to get ahold of you. She and my stepdad went to the service for Joey there in Texas. Below is a picture of the sign. I'm trying to figure out how to get one to anyone who wants one. The picture is actually a photo I took with my phone in Afghanistan. It just so happened that the picture is the bird that they were flying on that

night. I've been thinking of the guys a lot lately. This time of year is always rough for all of us. I think about them daily and tell stories about them all the time.

Your son used to hook me up with "Rare Flight Suits" all the time because of my height, 6'6 ½". Two weeks after the crash his shop found a flight suit hidden in the back with my name on it! It was my last "hook-up", and I still have that suit. Your son and his brothers are thought of all the time. We miss them. Thank you and your wife for raising such an honorable man.

Cpl. Boswell, James M. (Bos)

And this email came, as well:

Mr. Logan,
I am a Marine Corps Veteran, a Sergeant. I am so sorry for your loss. I didn't know Joey, nor was I a part of the Red Lions, but I was on location a few hours after the incident happened and there for several hours. I honestly have no idea what caused the incident; that is why I reached out to the Red Lions Project. However, I also do not want to upset you or your family. I can't imagine how difficult it must be. ... I am willing to talk if you are, but I'm extremely nervous. It is pretty much an unspoken rule for us to have communication with family members, as I was a member of the Personnel Retrieval and Processing Detachment—a very small and almost unknown MOS in the Corps.

I was also the Search and Recovery Team Leader for the incident on January 19th, 2012. I was injured during that mission and medically retired in 2013. My fire team also suffered indirect injuries, and we have all been searching for answers surrounding the cause of the crash for years with no success. Again, I am sorry for you and your family's loss...Your son and the rest of the Fallen Six were treated with the utmost honor, respect, and dignity a Marine could possibly bestow upon another Marine. We called them Heroes.

God bless and Semper Fi. Adam Sanders.

This light is from Ruth Neal Gonzales, an artist from Virginia, who created this stained glass proudly displaying the Red Lions logo.

At the Red Lions Project in Montana, you will find this light fixture, hanging on a cabin wall.

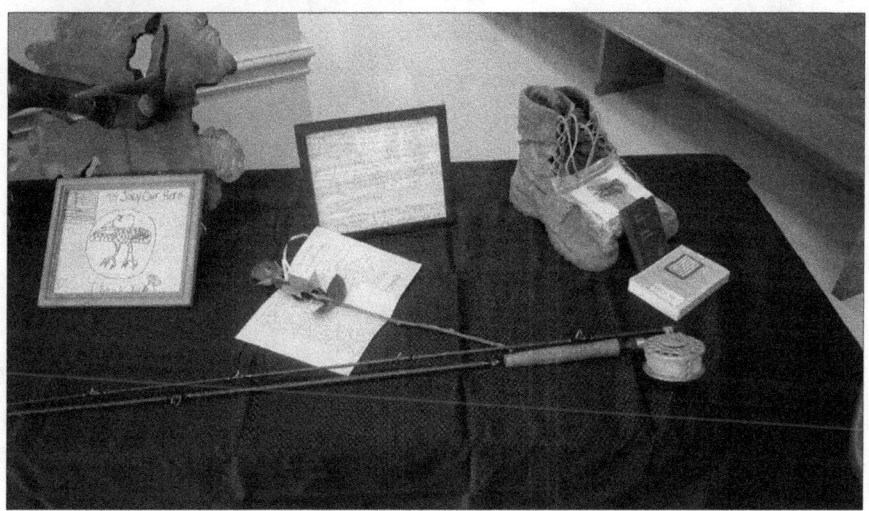

This photo includes memorabilia displayed at Joey's service, including his military bible, his fly rod, pictures drawn by students in the classroom of Joey's grade school teachers, combat boots, and an antelope horn trophy from his travels.

Front Row: Joaquin, Will, Bryan
Back Row: Mark, Ricky, Andy, Joey

Will, Joey, Ricky, Bryan and Evan in Afghanistan

After Joey passed, our family continued to receive letters from hundreds of honorable and loving patriots. I have kept them all and wish I could have responded to every one of them. The compassion expressed by all was overwhelming. I have a collection of these letters titled *Letters from Honorable Men.*

Because of the overwhelming grief and sadness, I will only mention the authors of the letters.

- Major General John H. Toolan is the general who pinned Joey's first Combat Air Medal on him in Afghanistan and gave him his challenge coin.
- Chief of Police, Houston Police Department, Charles A. McCelland Jr. (Chuck was my training instructor after I entered the police dept.)
- Lieutenant General Duane D. Thiessen, Pacific fleet Commander
- Lieutenant Colonel Mark Revor, Commanding Officer of HMH 363 Red Lions (Mark called us from Afghanistan the day they died).
- General Martin E. Dempsey U.S. Army, Chairman of the Joint Chiefs of Staff
- Ray Mabus, Secretary of the Navy
- General James F. Amos, Commandant of the Marine Corps
- Congressmen Bill Huizenga, from Michigan
- Ronald Davie, Blue Star Family Support Group
- Sergeant Major USMC Bryan Battaglia, Senior Enlisted Advisor to the Chairman of the Joint Chiefs of Staff
- Alan B. Sadler, Montgomery County, Texas Judge
- Congressmen Ted Poe

The correspondence from these people pales in comparison to the letters our family received from his fellow Marines with whom he served. They fought, sweated, and bled together, and I have tried to include as many of their letters as possible in this book. For me and all who read their writing, honoring the true essence of "Semper Fi" is a lasting tribute.

The statue we viewed at Audubon Park in New Orleans

Cpl. Joey Logan, with his usual friendly smile

About the Author

Thomas Logan grew up in a small town in upstate New York. During high school, he played three sports: Football, Baseball, and Track. He attended  college, earning a degree in Parks & Wildlife and Plant Science. During the Vietnam War, Tom enlisted in the United States Air Force for four years. He was a Small Arms Weapons instructor. He's always loved the outdoors, especially fishing and hunting.

Tom met his wife, Debi, while they were both on active duty. After being discharged, he served as a Houston police officer for 28 years. During that time, the Logans raised five children: Tommy, Robbie, Tricia, Joey, and Andi. Three of the Logan children entered the military.

Tom, who his wife affectionately calls a "Fishing Fool," orchestrated a once-in-a-lifetime surprise trip for his son after Joey's graduation. Both men had no idea what an adventure they were in for. Throughout their travels to nine states and two provinces in Canada, they caught over a million fish. They drove 16,000 miles, and only Debi knew their actual expenses! Shortly after returning from their wonderful trip, Joey headed off to basic training in the Marine Corps.

The Logans followed Joey throughout his military career, attending every school graduation he completed as he moved up the ranks. Their pride shone brightly when he finished first in his class and was selected to join the Marine Air Wing and become a crewmember flying in a CH-53 Super Stallion helicopter. Soon after, his training intensified, and the Logans were kept in the dark about his activities. During his next phone call, Joey informed them he was being deployed to Afghanistan to fight the war on terrorism. Like all parents, their hearts sunk at the prospect of a child going off to war.

When their son returned from his first deployment, Tom and Debi were thrilled to see how their son had matured. Sometime later, another call from him revealed his intention to go back. However, Joey's second tour ended in tragedy when his helicopter crashed while on a combat mission.

THE BIRTH OF THE RED LIONS PROJECT

Many hopes and dreams were shattered the night Joey died. Despite their loss, Tom and Debi aimed to turn things around and fulfill one of Joey's dreams. That led to the founding of the Red Lions Project in Montana.

Several months after Joey's death, the Logans traveled the same route that Joey and Tom had traveled on their infamous fishing trip. There were two reasons for the journey: 1) to spread some of Joey's ashes in places that he loved, and 2) to look for a final resting place in Montana where the Logans could build a cabin. They found both along the way. The Red Lions Project was subsequently established.

Shortly before his death, Joey shared his dream of purchasing land in Montana. His aim was to create a cabin in the mountains for fishing and hunting, providing a place for his Marine comrades to enjoy their favorite activities. Ultimately, the land was paid for with the money Joey had saved from two deployments to Afghanistan and with his life insurance policy. Joey had literally purchased a piece of heaven with his own blood. His memory and the Warrior Spirit will always be there.

The Logans decided they would put their grief into something productive to honor the Marines by using all 164 acres to build six cabins. In order to honor the Marines, they dedicated each cabin to one of the Fallen Six Heroes. Combat veterans can recover and revitalize at The Red Lions Project's retreat.

The property is completely surrounded by LoLo National Forest. The forest boundary covers 3,150 square miles of wilderness and forest access roads. It is in Mineral County, Montana. Eight miles away lies Superior, a small town with a population of just 900.

The town was founded when gold was first discovered in Montana. You can still pan for gold in the mountain streams. We have found gold and blue sapphires in our secret place. The town has a hotel and stores for supplies. The city of Missoula is located 60 miles east on Interstate 90. There is a major airport there, as well as a county airstrip near Superior.

If you love fishing as much as the Logans, the Clark Fork River is located only three miles from the property. Excellent trout fishing is available, and numerous mountain streams and lakes are nearby. The Idaho border is also close by. Hunting is an option for the outdoorsmen, with elk, deer, moose, bighorn sheep, mountain goats, wolves, and mountain lions available to hunt with the proper license.

The outdoor experiences are endless. If you want to relax in the beautiful mountains, it's all there for the ask. That is the goal and dream of the Project, and with the help of others, Joey's dream is coming true.

- Visit the Red Lions website: **www.redlionproject.org**
  or
- Email Tom Logan: **ltm2100@yahoo.com**

www.ingramcontent.com/pod-product-compliance
Lightning Source LLC
Chambersburg PA
CBHW081218170426
43198CB00017B/2648